Hiding In Death's Shadow

Hiding In Death's Shadow

✦

How I Survived The Holocaust; Second Edition

Allen Brayer

iUniverse, Inc.
New York   Bloomington

Hiding In Death's Shadow
How I Survived The Holocaust; Second Edition

iUniverse books may be ordered through booksellers or by contacting:

iUniverse
1663 Liberty Drive
Bloomington, IN 47403
www.iuniverse.com
1-800-Authors (1-800-288-4677)

ISBN: 978-1-4502-6382-5 (sc)
ISBN: 978-1-4502-6383-2 (ebook)

Printed in the United States of America

iUniverse rev. date: 11/08/2010

Contents

Acknowledgements

I would like to first and foremost acknowledge my children - Ron, Leora and Sheira for adding such an important dimension to my life, for their inspiration and for sharing and taking to heart all my stories throughout their entire lives. A special thanks to my daughter Leora, for tirelessly editing my book with her insight, creativity and above all patience; to my daughter Sheira for writing such a moving tribute and for proof-reading with her "eagle eyes". And thanks to my son, Ron, for offering support, inspiration and for your technical assistance.

I thank Mickie Schulman for being there for me throughout this arduous process, giving me encouragement along the way.

I thank Marcy Mechanic for helping out with the title of the book.

I express my appreciation to David Berg, Irving Weicher and Leo Gleicher for helping me piece together the details of my story. Thank you for your friendship all these years and for being my memory aids in the writing of this book.

I wish to recognize and honor the following gentiles who helped me to survive during a very dangerous time in my life: Joseph Markowitz and Nikolay Markowitz (no relation), and several others whose names I can no longer remember.

And, most importantly, I would like acknowledge the family that I lost - my mother, father, sister, cousins, aunts and uncles. I want you to know, wherever you are, that I have lived with the values and morals that you have instilled in me.

Dedication

I owe the writing of this book to my mother because if it weren't for her, it could not have been written. From the early days of my childhood, I had that special feeling that my mother loved me dearly. There is nothing that can compare to a mother's love. As horrible as my experience was, the memory of her love made it easier to endure. I think of her often. I have had this feeling always, that wherever she is, she has kept an eye on me. Many a time, even now, when I have something to share, I think of her subconsciously only to realize that she is not here. She is my inspiration and I know that her spirit lives on in me, in my children and in all the generations yet to come.

Introduction

I want you to know that my story will not be easy to tell. I am a Holocaust survivor. And even though I was lucky enough to be spared the concentration camps, I experienced a similar mind-numbing fear and an undeniable will to survive while hiding from the Nazis deep in the forests of the Carpathian Mountains.

I kept in many details about my life before the war because I wanted you to get to know me well so you could see all that I had, and all that I lost. Some stories you may find hard to believe and some details you may not care about, but I lived through it all. Even today I can well up with tears just thinking about everything I lost and all the horror I endured. And I have managed to make a life for myself despite Hitler's lofty goal of exterminating all the Jews. He couldn't fulfill his dreams because I'm still here. And so are my children and so are my grandchildren.

1

The Family

It was nearly the end of July in our small village of Radycz (pronounced: RA-ditch). The day started out peacefully, with the usual overwhelming worries. My mother, Hencia (pronounced: HEN-chya), and my sister, Manya, were returning home from a visit with family in the neighboring village Ilnik and became the messengers of disturbing news. When I saw them returning, I ran over to them and greeted them with warm hugs and kisses. I noticed, however, that mother was concerned about something. I knew my mother very well -- her smile, her demeanor, and her emotions. Mother attempted to minimize the news she was bringing with her. She revealed to me that the Germans have issued a directive: all the Jews from the surrounding villages have to report to Turka for resettlement to another place.

Mother gathered a few clothes for herself, my father, Akiva, and my little sister, Manya. The August weather was warm and they wouldn't need anything heavy. My Uncle Srul, one of the Judenrat (a Jewish Advisory Council), assured them they would be gone only a few hours, maybe just overnight. Uncle Srul and his brother-in-law, Moyshe Hans, lived only two miles away in the village of Ilnik. They were leaders in Ilnik's Jewish community of more than 50 families. My mother, father, sister, and I were the only Jews in the tiny village of Radycz.

Ours was one of the larger houses in the village, although it was a small, modest wooden farmhouse. There were a few other well-to-do Ukrainian farmers with large houses nearby, but most of the villagers lived in primitive wooden huts with dirt floors. For more than a year, our house had not been ours alone. The head of the village, Nikolay Markowicz, had taken over the front room for his office.

I don't mean to sound boastful, but I was very well educated at 14 years of age. Markowicz had asked me to help him out with the paperwork in the office because he, like the other farmers and peasants in the region, couldn't read or write.

Sensing the ever-increasing danger for Jews in the area, mother had asked Markowicz to get me the coveted "work permit". Since Markowicz was head of the village, it was no problem. Mother kept pressing him to get the *Arbeit* work permit for me which would guarantee me the desirable "A" on the armband, denoting preferential treatment. Although most of the work permits were for men working in the forest cutting timber, Markowicz saw the benefit of having me help out by doing the necessary paper work and he managed to obtain the desired "A" (*Arbeit)* work permit.

I didn't realize at the time that the "A" would help save my life, it just meant preferential treatment at the time – it turned out to be the single most important thing my mother ever did because it eventually allowed me to stay and work when others were being taken away.

Mother was uneasy about the transport to Turka where everyone was ordered to report to barracks built by the Russians the year before. It wasn't far, only four miles, and Markowicz had arranged transport as directed by the Germans two or three days before August 1, 1942.

The directive came down from the German High Command to the Judenrat as well as to the heads of all the villages surrounding the town of Turka. All Jews -- men, women and children -- without the letter "A" on their armband were to report with their immediate belongings to the army barracks on August 1 for resettlement to work in a labor camp. This new transport alarmed every Jew in the villages. For mother, however, there was a spark of hope.

Not only was I excused from reporting because of mother's successful plea for the permit, but also Uncle Srul assured our family that there was a special list of people who must report to the barracks, but would then be released to come home. My Uncle Srul's own wife and five-year-old daughter were on the list as well as our family. Also there was an important voice supporting the effort to free more Jewish families to work in the forest: a German voice – but not a Nazi. He was a local forester named Knopf who was trying to help the Jews in Ilnik who worked in the forest cutting timber and hauling it to the river for the German war effort. Knopf volunteered to negotiate with the Gestapo to have certain people on the list, including our family, returned to the villages to work in the forest for the war effort.

With several of our family members in the Judenrat and Uncle Srul assuring them that all would be well, mother resigned herself to traveling to Turka. She had no choice but to report to the barracks and hope to return home in the afternoon. I'm sure mother was relieved that I wouldn't have to leave Radycz.

The driver was waiting outside and mother joined father and sister Manya in the buggy. I remember standing alongside the buggy when I told mother that I don't want to be left alone, but she reminded me that someone must stay and take care of the house until they returned later in the day. She said there was hardly a question that they would be back, probably that afternoon.

I think mother saw the apprehension in my face despite her reassurances. So as not to alarm me I believe mother, in her loving way, fought to keep her own fears hidden as the driver urged his horse into a trot down the village, across the river Stryj (pronounced: STRAY), and ultimately to the barracks.

I walked a few steps following the buggy down the dirt road, then stood and watched as my family drove away. My mother's golden hair shone in the morning light, her summer dress bright next to my sister's dark hair. I wanted to go to with them to Turka but Mother said that I must stay and take care of the house.

The buggy carrying my family away from me wound past the last houses in our village and I lost sight as it turned left down the road. I could hear the horse's hooves on the road, then the sound faded. My heart was heavy but I convinced myself that we would have a happy reunion in just a few hours.

◆   ◆   ◆

Our village called Radycz was small; no more than 250 people. It was a rural village of farmers, peasants and forestry workers. It was where I was born and had lived all of my 14 years. Radycz was in Southern Poland in the rugged Carpathian Mountains near the Hungarian border to our south. There were other small villages within a few miles, all centered around the much larger town of Turka. The road to Turka ran right in front of our house dividing our farm; it was only a dirt road used mainly by the farmers and peasants in the area. Our house was number 8.

We spent most of our time in the kitchen, where a large stove kept us warm in the winter; there were always good smells coming from Mother's cooking. My parents slept in one of two bedrooms and my sister and I slept in the other. There was a living room, well lit with an open exposure overlooking the southern part of the village. No one spent much time in that living room but I used to sneak in there once in a while and look for all sorts of little things in the dresser drawers. Also, I would climb up to the attic and look at the fascinating things from World War I belonging to my father and one of my uncles.

Most of the houses were located on the farmland along the river, surrounded by forests in the distance. I call them houses but they were mainly primitive wooden huts with dirt floors. Most of the villagers were poor farmers whose huts consisted of one room most of which was taken up by an oven, and right next to it, or even a part of it, a stove. This served a dual purpose. It was used for baking and cooking and the flat top of the oven often served as a communal bed, especially in the wintertime when the temperature dropped below freezing. The winters in our mountains lasted from about October to May, with extremely cold temperatures and plenty of snow.

In Radycz and the other small villages, no one ever heard of a telephone or a radio. No one had electricity. Water for cooking and drinking came from the stream. There were no bathrooms or bathtubs or showers. I don't think any of the farmers ever took a shower. There was always a chance to take a dip in the river, but that wasn't practical in cold weather, especially in winter. In the summertime, children from the neighborhood would come and play in the river close to our house.

My father was a respected member of the village. He was a farmer, using the word loosely, and a part-time lumber broker. He wasn't a physically strong man so he had outside workers help with planting in the springtime and preparing for the harvest. We would cut the oats or wheat, tie it in bundles, and place it in storage to feed the cattle and our horse in the wintertime. Naturally, we cut plenty of wood for cooking and heating in the winter.

My mother was more involved with our three cows. The "mini" dairy farm was a rather modest operation. Mother had a woman who not only helped with the household chores and the running of the farm, but slept there too. Everyday, they milked the three cows early in the morning and processed the milk into butter, sour cream, and cheese. We also kept chickens, turkeys, ducks and geese as well as some sheep and goats.

To store the dairy products and keep the milk from getting sour, my father had a cold cellar built into a large hill close to the house. It served two purposes: in winter it was a storage place mainly for keeping potatoes, and in summertime it served as a refrigerator. Without electricity we had no way to cool things except by nature's way. The temperature of a cellar dug into the hill stayed cool and steady with little change between winter and summer. Earth provided good insulation either way.

Mother took pride in her cows' rich milk, golden butter and cheese. She was especially proud of her dairy's quality because the stores in town would fight over her products. Once a week on Sundays, my parents would hitch our horse to the buggy and take the dairy products to Turka. A modern town compared to the villages, Turka had brick houses, various shops, several nice bridges, electricity (if one could afford it) and a gas station. Occasionally, a car would pass -- perhaps once a week. The gas pump had to be operated manually and when it was in use, a crowd would gather to watch the process. Most of the transportation in and out of Turka was by horse-drawn vehicles or by train, which came through a tunnel into the local railroad station. The line ran through several small towns and then to a bigger city to the north—Lvov.

The horse we used to pull our wagon into Turka on Sundays was brown, and to a small boy, very tall. I recall watching my father shoe the horse and I tried to help him when I could. That was when our horse seemed so tall. It's not easy getting a big horse to pick up his foot so that you can pull off the old shoe. When I was eight or nine and bigger, my father let me shoe the horse but only under his supervision. That used to make me feel important and my father was proud of me.

It was also important to me that I help my father when I could. He was not well. Occasionally, he had problems with his heart as well as with his lungs.

When it came time to haul the manure into the fields, I was glad to do it and my father appreciated my help. Hauling the manure was one big job where I could be of help and work with our horse as well. With three cows, a horse, and many sheep and goats, we accumulated quite a pile of manure. Like most farmers we piled it behind the barn and covered it with tarps to keep it dry. When spring came the manure had cured into very good fertilizer that we spread on the land before planting crops of potatoes, oats, wheat and other grains. Mother used it in the little garden adjacent to the house where she grew strawberries, radishes, carrots, and onions—among other fruits and vegetables. My sister Manya and I always kept an eye on the strawberries, waiting for them to ripen. Across the road from the house was the stable for all the livestock. The chicken coop was there as well. Right next to the stable was the storage for hay, bundles of oats and wheat, which we placed in the attic and then threshed after the harvest was completed. With everything in dry storage we could continue threshing through the winter.

We were a rather religious family; I would say orthodox, but not fanatic. Every morning my father put on the *tefilin* (phylacteries) and *talis* (the prayer shawl) for prayers. He prayed in the evening as well. I used to wonder, as young as I was, how the non-Jews viewed this whole ceremony. I had strange feelings about being different. I liked to play with the kids in the neighborhood and wanted to be accepted as one of them, but I don't think I ever was. As I got a little older, about 7 or 8, they would tell me the Jews killed Christ but they didn't call me Christ killer. They told me the priest said it in Church, so they believed if the priest said it, it was indisputable. They would make fun of me about being circumcised and there were other derogatory comments.

When I was about three years old, my father started teaching me how to read and write in Yiddish with both the Hebrew and Polish alphabet. I would've rather played outside with the other kids but my father took education seriously. I went along for the ride, absorbing what I was taught -- not that I had a choice. My father didn't bother teaching my sister who was two years younger than I. Girls didn't have to be educated. The emphasis was on the son in every Jewish family. Because there was no school of any kind in our village, 99 percent of the villagers were illiterate.

When I was about five, my parents sent me to Turka to live in a couple's house, which served as a *cheder*, a parochial school. The man of the house was the teacher in the *cheder,* which was located in one of the rooms of his apartment. It was bad enough that I had to be away from home, but to be with that teacher 24 hours a day made it even worse. On Wednesdays, there was a bazaar in town, something resembling a flea market, but not exactly. Farmers from adjacent villages brought lumber to sell to the lumberyards in town. The money bought the basic necessities for home: salt, sugar (which was very expensive), gasoline for a lamp to illuminate a room or perhaps flour to bake white bread, which was a luxury. Some farmers would bring sheep, goats, chickens or eggs for sale. But the most popular were horses.

There was a big horse market in Turka where farmers could buy, sell or trade horses. Wherever there's a horse market there are, one might say brokers, who engage in trading horses. These brokers were very unscrupulous individuals. Fights would break out among them and the farmers. They often treated the farmers in a very undignified way, which became a source of anger and hatred towards the horse traders who were invariably Jewish.

Turka had many things to offer, but I would've gladly traded them in just to be home in Radycz. During the day I was in *cheder* learning and playing with other kids, but when the evening came I was very lonely. I missed my home very much, my parents, the little rocks and the trees; I missed it all. I worried about my parents. Who would be there to protect them if anything happened to them? My mind filled with thoughts of disaster. Some of the thoughts were pretty extreme.

Almost every Friday I managed to come home; either my parents would ask a farmer to pick me up if he happened to be in town or I would walk over to the bazaar place and ask for a ride home. Even at six or seven I would not miss the opportunity to come home. Otherwise, I stayed in town and eagerly waited for Sunday when my parents came to sell their dairy products. Seeing my parents was always a joyous occasion. When they came they always gave me money (equivalent to a nickel or dime), which I eagerly spent on ice cream or a bar of chocolate.

I always looked forward to coming home. I longed to see my parents but I also missed playing with the little animals on the farm, my dog, and also the neighborhood kids. There was so much to do in Radycz and so little fun in Turka. When I tired of playing with the little chicks or the turkeys I would go down to the river right by the house and spend hours playing along the banks. I used to watch the big guys fishing with their bare hands for trout, especially in the summertime. They would bring the catch over to my mother, she would buy it, and the way she prepared it was so indescribably delicious. Mother would clean it, fry it in butter and then serve it to us. There was nothing as delicious as those fish straight out of the cold mountain water; I can still smell it now.

I grew up fast on the farm. Children learn that certain things have to be done everyday without fail. Animals fed and watered, cows milked, crops planted and harvested; all these things cannot wait or be forgotten. One thing I learned early in life (that was a part of all farm life and a natural lesson for children) was the matter of sex. For example, with dairy cows you have to breed them to start their milk production. We didn't own a bull, so when a cow came into season, my father would bring another farmer's bull to the cow. I used to watch the whole process as the bull would mount the cow and perform the service that my father paid the other farmer for. Somehow I learned the whole thing naturally and didn't have to ask questions about what the bull was doing.

There was no need to hide and watch the mating of the cattle or the other animals on the farm. It was a natural thing and not something that fascinated me. What did fascinate me was superstition. There was a lot of superstition in the village. Even my mother believed in superstition. I'm not sure whether she really believed in it. Maybe she told herself "it may not help, but it can't hurt."

Superstitious people believed that an evil spirit, better known as the evil eye, caused most ills. Mother had the most interesting way of breaking this evil spirit. If a cow wasn't well or someone had a headache, she would place a clove of garlic on the ground. She had me pick it up and take it about five houses down the road to a neighbor who was able to break the evil spirit.

When I got to the neighbor's house I placed the garlic clove on the ground, never handing it to the neighbor directly. Not a word was spoken but somehow he knew what I was there for. The neighboring farmer with the miraculous power over the evil eye, Juzio Markowicz would then pick up the garlic from the ground and go behind the house or behind a tree, out of sight. I was very interested to find out what he was doing, but I wouldn't dare interfere with the process so I never witnessed the conquering of the evil spirit. He would spend a few minutes there and then reappear, placing the garlic on the ground. I would then pick up the garlic and take it back to my mother repeating the procedure. Mother would pick up the garlic and take it to the cow or individual with the headache, circle the sufferer's face clockwise three times and "the ailment would be gone." If not, then the ailment was not due to the evil eye (wink, wink). Mind you, my mother was a religious woman and yet she somehow believed in superstition. As young as I was, I was skeptical about the whole situation, but I wouldn't contradict my mother or even question it because I loved her too much and I felt a reciprocal feeling from her. I respected her; she was my friend.

It was a little different when the person suffering the headache was a family member. Mother was able to determine whether the headache was due to the evil eye or to other reasons. She would take a cup of cold water and throw in a hot coal from the stove. If the water gave out a hissing noise, which it normally would, my mother would identify if the evil eye was responsible or not. It all depended on the kind of noise the hot coal generated. Usually a loud hiss confirmed the evil eye.

Country ways and plain common sense answered many situations. My mother had ways of solving problems that had nothing to do with superstition; we call it "practicing medicine without a license." If an eyelash or something got into my eye, my mother would use the moist tip of her tongue in a very delicate way to wipe over my eyeball dislodging it. Her agile but gentle tongue removed it and she spit it out. It always worked like a charm. I loved my mother.

Being away from my mother was difficult for both of us but I knew, even at seven, that education was more important than anything else. It was still a painful experience to live in Turka without her kind and loving companionship.

In Poland, the law requires that every child upon reaching seven years of age must attend school. This applied to all children living in towns or cities where there were schools. It applied to me as I was living in Turka. Because my father taught me how to read and write early in life, and later sent me to *cheder*, when I reached seven I was advanced beyond my years and was put in the fourth grade. I found myself with guys older and taller than I was and I didn't like it at all!

I don't know what else my parents could've done. I'm sure they meant well. For them, education was paramount, almost at any cost; but I was the one who had to pay. They didn't look at the psychological aspect of the situation. It was the Polish school in the morning and in the afternoon the *cheder,* which lasted most of the time till late in the evening, especially in the wintertime when it would get dark very early. This was a difficult time for me. I was so alone. I missed my family terribly. The local children were able to go home to their families; I didn't have that luxury. I had no choice. I accepted that arrangement even though I wasn't too pleased with it because I trusted my parents, especially my mother whom I loved dearly. For her, I made the best of it.

I would often come home for the weekend – a very pleasant experience, but I had to be back in school Monday morning -- a dreadful thought. Most of the time, I stayed home over Sunday night. The consequence was that I had to get up at 5am Monday morning so I could be in school at 8:30. It was worth the sacrifice even though only God knew how difficult it was to get up that early. When it was winter, everything was dark and cold at 5am. I slept so cozily under a soft, thick comforter made by my mother, who plucked the down from very our own geese. Mother would come into my room very reluctantly to wake me up with a sweet kiss. It probably hurt her as much as it hurt me to get up. Then I had the four mile walk from Radycz to Turka if I went the regular way. There was a short cut, though, over a mountain, which cut the distance in half (if there was no snow). Even when I was a small boy starting out before dawn and sometimes in heavy fog, I had no fear. There was never any incident of a crime; that's why fear never entered my mind.

When I was about eight years old, while attending the Polish school I was placed in a more advanced *cheder*. The emphasis at that *cheder* was the five books of Moses. Every week there was another chapter of the book to be translated from Hebrew to Yiddish. The five books of Moses have fifty-four chapters that coincide with the Hebrew year so that one encounters the same part of the bible translation once a year. That method of teaching was rather counter- productive. We students invariably forgot the translation and had to start all over again the following year. Instead, they should've taught Hebrew as a language, then we wouldn't have had to repeat the translation year in and year out. There was a severe price to pay for not knowing the translation. Every student had to know the translation by Thursday. If we didn't, we had to face the consequences. One of the things we looked forward to was our short play period when we could let off steam and get away from our teacher. It didn't matter what games we played as long as we had a break. We used to play with buttons trying to flip them into a hole or a game similar to baseball but without a ball using short sticks instead. If you didn't know your translation you forfeited the privilege of playing outside. In the worst cases, the punishment could go as high as being beaten with a *kuncik*, a leather strap especially designed for that purpose.

If we had liked our teacher we might have been less likely to try and get even, but he wasn't a very nice man. He was downright nasty at times. Our teacher was an elderly man who was too serious and too self-involved. He wasn't too aware of what was happening around him. In spite of the respect that my parents demanded and the respect they expected me to show my elders, I couldn't help but enjoy the tricks my fellow students pulled on our teacher. One day, the guys put a piece of poison ivy in his jacket sleeve. Right after lunch, when it was time to teach again, he would put on his jacket and encounter the poison ivy and the rest was painful. No one ever squealed.

Another time a student took a small wooden board, the size of a seat, hammered a few nails into it so that they protruded on the other side. When the teacher sat down on the chair – ouch! The teacher always tried to find out who did these terrible things, but everyone kept the secret. Our frustration got the best of us.

All week I would look forward to Saturday—just to be home. But the problem was that Saturday is the Jewish Sabbath. Being observant Jews, my parents would not allow us to do anything to disturb the

Sabbath. Manya and I did not like the passive life on the Sabbath. We couldn't pick berries, or climb a tree to get apples or pears. We couldn't swim, or ride the horse or fish, among other things. One Saturday, Manya and I were just walking along the river when I spotted a trout in the water. I thought I could catch that trout but I wasn't allowed to. What was a little kid to do? Make a deal with his little sister. And that's exactly what I did. I told Manya that I would catch the trout and hide it in a secluded place until the Sabbath was over. Manya agreed and I set about catching the trout. I found a place in the river where it couldn't be seen unless you knew where to look. Then I placed some rocks in the shallow water so that the trout could swim around but couldn't escape.

Sunday morning came and I retrieved the still lively trout and brought it into the house pretending that I had just caught it. Mother cleaned it and we had a delicious lunch. She was so proud of me and it felt great. Then I got into an argument with my sister and guess what? She spilled the beans. I expected more than just a reprimand but it turned out to be rather mild—my mother just loved me too much and I always felt it. I don't think she had the same strong feelings for my sister but, I believe, my father did.

I didn't need Manya's tattletales to get me in trouble. Sometimes we underestimated our abilities and literally fell into a bad situation. One time, when I was only seven and Manya, five, when we tried to fool Mother. She would bake only once a week—on Friday mornings. On Thursday, she started kneading the dough, leaving it to rise overnight, so it could be ready for baking on Friday. Bread was an important part of our meals but it was the cookies we were interested in. Mother's sugar cookies were divine.

Learning from the past, my mother knew if she left those cookies unattended, they would probably not last too long. We would always steal some, leaving enough and hoping mother wouldn't discover the theft. On one occasion, when she had to leave us alone, Mother placed the cookies high up in the cabinet out of the reach of childish hands. Little genius that I was, I designed a scheme. I took a chair and put another chair on top of it. Manya was supposed to hold the chair so that it didn't slip; it was a joint effort. My job was to climb up and get the cookies. Unfortunately, the plan failed. The chair slipped and I fell on my back and couldn't catch my breath for quite a while. I recovered, but no cookies. I don't think my mother knew what had happened when she returned.

Since there were no other Jews in Radycz, there was no formal place to pray. One needs ten Jewish men for a *minyan* – otherwise there's no service. Occasionally my father would go to Ilnik to pray in the house of his cousin. Only two miles away, Ilnik was a much larger village with a much larger Jewish population, perhaps forty or fifty families. Although there was no formal synagogue, they did have *schtibls*. A *schtibl* was usually located in a Jewish house that could accommodate a good number of people and was used in lieu of a synagogue. Moyshe Hans, who was a cousin probably twice or three times removed, had such a *schtibl* in his house in Ilnik. Moyshe Hans' sister Gitl was married to my uncle Moyshe-Avrum who lived next door. Little did I know that years later this house would play a pivotal role in my life.

Every year, my family would spend the High Holidays with my relatives, usually with Uncle Moyshe-Avrum. We would pray next door in Moyshe Hans' house, men and women in separate rooms. I personally didn't like the discipline of the holidays (especially the praying!).

At seven years old, I had no interest in sitting among grown-ups or watching them pray and cry. It was a depressing sight, to say the least. I would've preferred to be outside, but my father was rather strict. This might explain why I don't particularly care for prayers.

Not all holidays were spent in Ilnik. Sometimes Mother, Manya and I stayed home and Father went alone. On one Passover morning, my parents got up early. Father was getting ready to walk to Ilnik to pray in the *schtibl* and Mother got up to make breakfast. Manya and I loved to get into our parents' beds. They were single beds with a night table in between. My sister would occupy mother's bed and I would jump into my father's bed.

I don't know why, but my father left his handgun in the upper drawer of the night table. My father had a permit to carry a gun. I think there were rumors that certain farmers might be stealing hay so father kept the gun for protection. At any rate, being as curious as I was, I pulled out the drawer and there it was—the gun. It was equivalent to a 45 and rather heavy, especially for a seven-year old kid. When I saw it, I must have said, "Wow".

I was fascinated by the gun and would watch my father clean it. Because I had watched him, I felt I could handle the gun no problem. Once or twice, when the gun was empty, my father would allow me not only to hold it but to pull the trigger. And I did.

Manya watched me hold our father's gun. Trying to show off, I said, "I know how the gun works". I had no clue that the gun was loaded. I tried to aim at Manya. Fortunately, the gun was so heavy that I couldn't hold it, aim it, and pull the trigger all at once. The gun wobbled slightly to the side as I pulled the trigger. There was a tremendous bang. All hell broke loose: the smoking gun, the surprise, the fear and everything else connected with it, including making in my pants. The bullet hit the side of the bed where my sister was lying, went through the door and smashed into a rock in the wall.

My parents reluctantly walked into the bedroom, expecting the worst. Pretty sure that I would be crucified, I was relieved and surprised that my parents didn't mention any punishment. I'm sure they were happy that both of their children were alive. My father probably felt guilty leaving the gun where he did. It certainly sobered me up a lot and accelerated the process of maturing. I felt very bad for my mother, having put her through this horrific ordeal.

Nothing I ever learned in school taught me more than the lesson I learned at seven with that gun. There would be other lessons learned that would speed my maturity in a life-altering way.

◆   ◆   ◆

After my parents and sister left that afternoon, I would imagine over and over in my mind how things must have gone: The road into Turka was familiar to them. My family had made the trip almost every Sunday as far back as I could remember. Today, however, it was different. It was a Sunday unlike any other; there were no dairy products to sell. Mother brought only small parcels of personal belongings as instructed by the German authorities. Nothing could relieve the tension in mother's mind and she was sure that her husband felt it too. My sister Manya, sitting beside mother, was probably not as aware of the danger they were in, but must've kept quiet realizing that there was nothing that could be done, except hoping that something may materialize with respect to the list.

The usual bustling streets must have seemed sinister as the buggy moved toward the barracks. Away from their friendly Ukrainian neighbors, my parents must've sensed the hostility from the more militant Ukrainians who seemed to be full of hatred standing on the side and watching what was happening to the Jews. The nationalistic Ukrainians hated everyone else, the Poles, the Russians, and especially the Jews. They were capable of killing their enemies without a second thought and had proved it.

In the afternoon that my parents and sister drove away I finished what work I had in Markowicz' office. The sun was behind the mountains, the boss had gone home to his farm, and I was alone with my memories of how we'd come to this day. The melancholy of dusk, of being lost and so alone, overwhelmed all of my thoughts, except one.

Where was my family?

◆　　◆　　◆

2

Betrayal

By late afternoon, I began to look for some indication that my parents and Manya were coming home. It seemed strange that they were in Turka and I was home in Radycz, so unlike most of my life when it had been the other way around. My parents knew that the time spent in study was not wasted and, now that I was 14, I understood as well. Watching my boss Markowicz, I couldn't help thinking how sad it was that a grown man, who was not stupid, could exist without knowing how to read and write. Outside our tiny village, the world was tearing itself apart and I realized that he knew only what others told him. Sometimes I was the one who brought the news from Turka.

Who would bring the news from Turka now? Uncle Srul? I had not heard from Uncle Srul. I knew that he and other members of the Judenrat were working to get work permits, bargaining with the Gestapo and arranging that the people on the list be returned to their villages to work in the forest not transported to an unspecified work camp. With his own family on the list I was sure that he would see that they, and my family, returned safely.

Each sound of horses' hooves sent me to the door but disappointment just made the waiting harder. A sense of anxiety crept into my mind gnawing at my resolve to stay calm. The lack of information about what was happening in Turka ate away at my confidence. In a way, I knew too much about recent events in Poland.

◆   ◆   ◆

From the age of seven I had been in classes with older children. That, and the Jewish tradition of education, probably led to me learning faster. In Turka, we heard gossip and rumors, read newspapers and heard radio broadcasts all talking about the turmoil in Europe. It was part of our history classes. In school I became aware of the different countries and their economies. Naturally, Polish history was important and the years since the First World War had given us students much to learn. I lived in what the Austrians called Eastern Galicia when it was part of the Austrian-Hungarian Empire. After the end of the war Poland regained that territory as well as a corridor to the port of Gdansk on the Baltic in the north. Without that piece of land, Poland was a landlocked country depending only on rail and river traffic for trade beyond its borders. From our history lessons it seemed to me that everyone always wanted another piece of Poland. In fact, a couple of hundred years earlier, the whole country had been divided up between Russia, Prussia and Austria. Our history teachers made sure that we knew that most of that land had been returned.

Everyone still wanted the Polish land, everyone being Russia and Prussia, which was now a state in Germany. Even after treaties ended the First World War, the Poles and the Russians continued to fight over territory, sometimes with guns—always with words.

People were beginning to talk about Adolph Hitler and his hate for the Jews. The Germans were determined to get back all that they had lost and Poland held the prize. The Polish newspapers wrote about Hitler's annexation of Austria and a year later Czechoslovakia, with the consent of the British and the French. While all this was happening, Hitler kept on talking about the northern part of Poland and the port of Gdansk, which is what the Germans called Danzig. Hitler claimed that Danzig and the corridor that split the German state of Prussia into East and West Prussia, belonged to Germany. I was keenly aware of the political situation. I was growing up fast and I was very much involved in current events. I read newspapers and was aware of the situation and of a possible war.

The war clouds began to appear darker and darker every day. When I couldn't get a ride home from Turka, I used to walk across the mountains and pastures. Farmers working in the fields would stop me and ask questions about what was happening in the world. They thought that coming home from the big town, I had the most up-to-date information.

The Jewish population was preoccupied and endlessly discussing the tense situation. Everyone was hungry for news, any news, especially good news. Early in 1939, Markowicz, the head of our village acquired a radio, probably the first radio in the history of Radycz. One of the voices I heard is still vivid in my mind. It was Adolph Hitler speaking in a loud, demagogic voice, threatening Poland that he must have the northern part of Poland connecting Germany with Prussia. The President of Poland, Smigly-Rydz also spoke on the radio telling Hitler that Poland will not cede any territory and that Poland will fight him to the last man, to the last drop of blood. Then we heard that England and France threatened that if Hitler attacks Poland, they will immediately declare war on Germany. As I was listening to the radio on a few occasions Hitler had a field day threatening the Jews for all the terrible things they had done to the Germans. He also said that the threat voiced by England and France was a Jewish conspiracy. Not that the Poles were so fond of the Jews, but the words coming out of Hitler's mouth sounded much, much worse. It made my stomach turn inside out coupled with an agonizing fear and an unknown tomorrow.

The Ukrainians, living in a large part of the area, disliked the Poles. They saw Poland as an occupying power and perhaps rightfully so, but then the Ukrainians, who thought they should be an independent country, disliked the Russians as well. Poland was recreated in 1918 after the collapse of the Austrian Empire and Polish sovereignty was recognized over the area, including Turka, which was largely inhabited by Ukrainians. As much as the Ukrainians disliked the Poles, they hated the Jews even more. Also, many poorer and ignorant people thought that all Jews were rich. I knew that wasn't so. We certainly weren't rich but we were educated and that mattered—and then there were the religious teachings of the churches that Jews had killed Christ.

The Jew was considered an alien, even though he lived in the area for generations; to the poor, the Jew was an exploiter and a millionaire; to the patriots the Jew was a man without a country; to all other classes a hated rival. The propaganda that Hitler and his lieutenants were spewing only exacerbated the whole situation.

It looked very much like war was imminent. The Jews, in the meantime, felt very threatened not knowing what to expect. My family felt the same way, but we just went on with our daily routines and hoped for the best. The local Jewish population in the villages constantly discussed the situation. As bad as it sounded, most didn't anticipate the worst nor did they consider leaving. Some families did leave earlier. In Galicia, our area, the Zionist movement was influential and strongly advocated immigration to Palestine in 1936. They had no illusions about the fate of the Jews in Europe. One family, the Singers, husband, wife and three children went to Palestine and settled in Natanya. The other Jews thought that it was a heroic act, but no one else entertained the idea of leaving nor did anyone predict what was to come.

There was one spark of hope, which made the outlook for the future somewhat brighter. We all thought that the declaration of support for Poland from Britain and France would have a sobering effect on Herr Hitler not to start a war. We always counted on an added factor as a back up, namely America. That added greater favorable odds to this political game, or so we thought.

Like most events that you have no control over, the turmoil outside our little village increased in ways that we couldn't see. On the farm, each day was almost a copy of the day before. The sun rose, we set about doing our usual farm chores, Mother saw that her three cows were milked and everything was put away in the cool of the cellar. My father said prayers, and I, if away at school, studied.

I was 11 and I was home from school. It was Friday -- the day before the Sabbath. It was the day that my mother baked the bread. Mother sent me on an errand to another farm outside our village.

Out of the west and out of nowhere I saw many airplanes racing across the sky toward the east. I stopped and watched, unable to see clearly enough which planes they were. A few minutes later more planes showed up and started to bomb the railroad and tunnel in Turka. As the planes released the bombs, anti-aircraft guns fired at the planes throwing shells into the air that exploded into black puffs. This gave the effect that there were more planes than there actually were. I had never experienced anything like that before. It was September 1, 1939, and the word spread fast that we were at war.

I ran home telling my mother what I had seen and saw the fear in her eyes. She had been a child during the First World War but she was old enough to know what was going on and the terrible toll on families. Why did we have to live in such fear? Every Jewish family must have gathered around that night and talked about what would happen next. We couldn't have imagined how different things would be in a month.

We knew nothing about the secret non-aggression pact between Hitler and Stalin signed the week before—a pact that hacked Poland in two like a slaughtered steer, one side to the Nazis and the other to the Soviets. We were living in a butchered carcass that was once a proud and peaceful country. The vultures were circling.

Germany and Russia agreed to divide Poland between them. Hitler had made good on his threat. Germany would occupy the western part and, naturally, the Soviet Union would take over the eastern part. The Polish army, which had a few planes, some tanks and mostly horse-drawn artillery, was no match for the German panzers. The German Luftwaffe attacked Polish airfields and destroyed most of the Polish Air Force on the ground. On September 17, 1939, the Soviet Army invaded Poland from the east. Within two weeks Poland was no more.

The Germans entered Turka, stayed a day and a half and moved out to leave the area to the Soviets as per agreement. The Jewish population in Turka and surrounding areas began to worry and to realize the seriousness of the situation. No one knew how serious it was going to be. Our little village, tucked into a corner of what was once Poland was awash with hatred. The Ukrainians, who welcomed the Germans, suddenly were back in the hands of the hated Russians. Their freedom from the equally hated Poles was short-lived.

Just the opposite happened to the Jews when the Soviet army entered the area. They sighed with a great deal of relief. The army itself was a sight to behold. They came with horses dragging their wagons with food and ammunition, the shabbily dressed soldiers made a very poor impression. One thing that stood out, rather noticeably, was their propaganda. It was probably as good as the German propaganda, if not better.

The Soviets started out by saying, almost immediately, that they came to liberate every one, except the rich and those that oppressed the masses. To the Jews, that sounded like sweet music. Some Jews began to worry about the definition of rich. If one was rich, or politically undesirable, the Soviets had a special way to handle it. The police would order the head of the community to have a horse and buggy available for a special hour, usually late in the evening. They would pull up in front of the dwelling of the targeted person, wake up the entire family, read them the order that they are being resettled. The family would just disappear; the next day no one would know what happened and no one would talk about it.

It was very scary. My mother would quietly express her concern, because compared to others, we had some money. Obviously the Soviets didn't consider us in either the rich or politically undesirable category. If they had, our family would have gone through a great deal of hardship during and after the resettlement.

Within a few months after France and England declared war on Germany, France was defeated. This was around June 1940. I read newspapers about how France fell to the German *Blitzkrieg* within a short period of time. Just like Poland, except that we thought the French army was much stronger. The sudden fall of France was frightening and unexpected. Little by little, Hitler and his invincible army swallowed up most of the countries in Europe. England was still struggling, but many questioned how long the British could hold out.

America was oceans away, unprepared for any major confrontation to stop Hitler, who, at this point, was confident that he was on the way to creating a "new order" that would last 1000 years. We Jews, in frustration, couldn't understand what was happening. I felt that it was almost a matter of time before Hitler's plan of conquest would materialize. He appeared to be unstoppable. Worst of all, we heard stories about the atrocities that the Gestapo was perpetrating on the Jews. The whole situation was terrifying.

While Hitler's armies were conquering Europe, the Soviets were trying to conquer our minds, constantly bombarding the population in the villages with their propaganda, about their five-year economic plans. They drummed into our ears how they will overtake the United States economically and politically. They claimed the communist system is the only system that will survive and that all the other systems were doomed. It worked for a while, but then the people began to have doubts and realized that it was all propaganda. As long as one kept his nose clean or better still, showed support and enthusiasm for the Soviet system, one could go places. A cooperative person would be able to get a better job, be promoted, or perhaps do a little spying on his friends or relatives and thus acquire power. Some Jews of the younger generation—in their early twenties—took advantage of it.

We noticed a change even in our small village. Under the Polish administration, we Jews were looked down upon, treated like second class citizens. All of sudden the new Soviet administration proclaimed that every citizen has equal rights. Unlike before, a Jew now could be an official, work in an office, be an officer. The Soviets even proclaimed that Jews should not be called *zyd*, a derogatory expression, and that a Jew should be called *Yevrey*, which in Russian means Hebrew.

The Germans and Soviets might appear to be friendly but they really didn't trust each other and it became apparent to those of us who had some knowledge that the alliance wouldn't last. Turka was not too far from the newly created border between Germany and the Soviets. The Soviets suddenly started to install telephone lines in Turka and all the surrounding villages. The population living in villages very close to the border was evacuated and transported lock stock and barrel hundreds of miles away close to the Soviet's old border with Poland. The border had a wide strip of empty land, which was presumably done for security reasons.

The Soviets didn't exactly see eye-to-eye with the United States. Capitalism, they believed, couldn't co-exist with communism and it was only a matter of time before capitalism would vanish from the face of the earth. The propagandists bragged about the Soviet Union overtaking the United States economically within a short period of time. I personally didn't think that they believed it, but the speeches were very patriotic and persuasive.

All that seemed far in the future as written by Stalin while in our corner we saw something else. The Soviets bought out all the goods from the stores at very cheap prices and put many stores out of business because the storekeepers could not replenish the merchandise. There were no goods to be gotten because of severe shortages in the Soviet Union. Our family's lives were really not too affected by the regime. We were more concerned about Hitler and his henchmen perpetrating all sorts of atrocities against the Jews. The newspapers were describing the actions and reporting the speeches by Hitler as well as his minister of propaganda, Herr Joseph Goebbels.

The villagers didn't show their resentment towards the Jews openly, but we could tell how pleased they were with Hitler's propaganda. Plus, they disliked the Soviets and many blamed the Russian occupation on the Jews.

Rumor had it that the Soviet Union would attack Germany, perhaps realizing that Hitler would eventually turn on them. One would think that the Soviets would be better prepared for such an eventuality.

3

Background to Slaughter

The day ended without the release of my family but the promise of the list remained that they definitely would be released tomorrow. It was the only possibility and didn't apply to all—only those few on the list. The people on the list were being freed to work here in the forest. The rest of the Jews in the barracks had no hope for release, but the whole idea of this move, the Germans said, was to transport these Jews for resettlement in another area for work—work for the German industry. I couldn't sleep thinking about Mother and how discouraged she must be having to spend the night at the Russian barracks.

The days of the Soviet occupation had been strange but not as terrifying as what we were experiencing now. In June of 1941, it wasn't obvious to us or even Stalin himself that Hitler would break their pact. I had just turned 13 in April. Russian propaganda was everywhere and we were used to the same words over and over about communism defeating the West and how decadent the Americans were. I don't remember the Soviets saying anything bad about the Germans who were the Russians' mortal enemies before they banded together to carve up Poland. The only sign that the comrades were getting nervous was the clearing of the land around the border and the installation of telephones in, what the Soviets thought would be, frontline areas. The Russians had installed the telephones about a year before for the purpose of alerting the authorities in case of an emergency because all of the villages were situated not far from the new German border created after Hitler and Stalin swallowed up Poland.

The Russians installed a telephone for Markowicz in our house. Since a number of phones were installed in adjacent villages all hooked up on the same line, a call from the main switchboard in Turka would reach all of the villages. Anyone on the phone could hear the conversation even if it didn't apply to that particular village. I couldn't prove it but I imagined that there was a lot of shouting when more than one Ukrainian or Russian got on the line at the same time.

On June 22, 1941, Hitler surprised Stalin and attacked exactly at 4:00 am. Suddenly, we were in the middle of a war once again. Employing the *blitzkrieg*, which had worked so effectively in Poland, the Germans completely overwhelmed the Soviet forces. Within three or four months, the German Army was at the gates of Moscow.

When the Germans attacked the Soviet Union, they attacked from the north and from the southeast in the area where we lived in order to cut off the Soviets and thus trap them. The Soviets were ill prepared and surprised by the sudden attack. Recognizing the situation they were in, the Soviet army units evacuated almost overnight to avoid being surrounded by the Germans. This created a vacuum in our part of the country.

In a shrewd and calculated move, Hitler promised the Ukrainians, who had no love for the Soviets whom they considered an occupying power, that he would establish an independent Ukraine. That promise achieved its goal when many of the Red Army units (consisting predominantly of Ukrainians led by a charismatic nationalist known as Bandera) simply capitulated, surrendering to the Germans. The final blow came when Bandera's units then volunteered to turn on their former comrades and fight the Soviets. Then, in another calculated and more sinister move, the Germans didn't bother to move in to set up an occupying administration. Instead they bypassed the entire area and left the management of the communities to the local population—the Ukrainians.

As the Red Army desperately abandoned the area, the Jews in Eastern Galicia faced a quandary. Everything was happening at lightning speed. No one had thought of this possibility and was not prepared for any action. Should they move out and follow the Soviets or stay and let another conqueror claim the area until a new force came yet again. We rationalized that as simple folk we were not involved in politics and the troubles would blow over as they had in World War I. Generally, civilians weren't harmed. Some of the most violent days for Jews came from the Poles themselves immediately after Poland achieved independence in 1918. The pogroms terrorized the Jewish population until the next wave of soldiers came from the east in 1920 when the Soviet Bolsheviks invaded and brought their own pogroms. Despite the terror of the recent past, all through the area Jews deliberated whether to move out and follow the Soviets. The few Jews who decided to flee east were those who held positions in the Soviet administration or were otherwise vulnerable. Hardly entertaining the idea of leaving their homes and whatever little they possessed, the rest of the Jews—the artisans, farmers, plain ordinary people—remained.

We were naïve. Yes, we heard the stories about the notorious Hitler's *Mein Kampf,* his concentration camps, the killings, but we didn't know the extent of our danger. Wars had washed over these mountains so many times that people lost count. No one visualized, believed, or predicted what was to come. The ordinary Jew didn't want to believe, because we didn't want to admit it or do anything about it. Obviously we were more than naive. If any of us had known—had seen the imminent danger—we would have dropped everything and left. The peril was closer than we knew and at this point there was little we could do about it.

The Ukrainians had waited for this moment for decades and took advantage of the vacuum left by the retreating Soviets and absent Germans. They took their role to manage the local communities very seriously. Having gotten rid of the hated Soviets, and having embraced Hitler as their liberator, they felt free to take matters into their own hands.

The Nazi dictator had promised the Ukrainians their own independent country and, of all those who oppressed them all these years, the Ukrainians blamed the Jews for all their troubles. Now that they had the power, there was no one to challenge them. The first thing on the agenda was the Jewish 'problem'. They set about solving "this problem" with great joy and enthusiasm…even if it meant brutally murdering their neighbors.

In all the surrounding villages the Ukrainians -- whether poor, rich, old, or young -- took part in an organized massacre of the Jews. The pogrom swept up thousands of ordinary Ukrainians, some watching, some helping to round up Jews who tried to escape. They took away their possessions and killed them indiscriminately, some using clubs, rocks, knives—whatever they had at their disposal. This was done with such tremendous hatred and anger, it was just indescribable that one human being can do this to another.

Much to our surprise, our immediate area was relatively quiet. Some Ukrainians took pleasure in describing the slaughter in other villages. We heard all these terrible stories about the atrocities taking place so close to home, and were extremely concerned about our safety. How ironic that Jews were praying for the Germans to move in and stop the bloodshed. We knew what the Germans stood for, but we thought once they moved in they would establish 'order'.

Fortunately there were decent people who lived in the adjacent villages in our community. The Jews in our villages had a pretty good relationship with the local Ukrainian neighbors. That didn't mean that they loved the Jews; they just wouldn't resort to this type of behavior.

One day during the time of the Ukrainian slaughter, several individuals came from those remote villages where the atrocities were taking place. Whether they were just passing through or deliberately came to have some 'fun' with the Jews, I didn't know. Several of our neighbors came over to make sure that no harm would come to us. When two of the strangers came to our house they began bragging in great detail to the local Ukrainians how they took part in the killing of Jews.

My mother pretended that she didn't hear their discussion. But she heard every word and managed to get out of the house to tell me to go and hide—just disappear from sight. I understood exactly what she meant even though she didn't go into details. It was a beautiful day, sunny and pleasant, but as I slipped away quietly to a farmer's house close by. Everything seemed unreal, dark and frightening. From their attic, I watched the children play and saw the farmers with their wives out in the street without a shred of fear. It was hard to accept it. It's amazing how quickly a boy of 13 grows up -- almost in an instant.

All my young life I felt that I was different—different religion, different language. The Ukrainian and Polish children made me aware of other details. They called me all sorts of names. I was a Christ killer, first of all, a crime for which I couldn't be absolved. "I had nothing to do with that," I would tell them but their answer would always be the question, "Are you not a Jew?" That seemed to be all the evidence they needed. I was condemned and it wasn't open to discussion. The non-Jewish kids called me circumcised for fun or *zyd,* the Polish word for Jew and a derogatory term, just to antagonize me. Whatever they did I always had the feeling I didn't belong. This wasn't my country and it never would be. It's a horrible feeling to not belong, to not feel like part of a community.

The Germans finally moved into town and established 'order' by publishing the usual Proclamation by the German high command that everyone is to obey the rules. With 'order' established they moved with lightning speed and efficiency. The sight of a German spelled fear in a big way. There was something about them, the way they walked, the way they talked; they definitely appeared as though they were representing a super race.

Among their rules and regulations was an order that Jews must wear a white armband with a blue Star of David. The Jews must also select a Judenrat to represent them and Jewish Police to keep order. These two organizations wore yellow armbands and 'enjoyed' certain privileges—like freedom of movement and a false sense of security. Some liked the feeling of being important, and, there were those who took this whole situation very seriously. It was clever the way the Germans set up the whole operation by having Jews help annihilate their own kin—very clever.

Most members of the Judenrat, as well as the Jewish Police, got involved for several reasons. Some had no choice; they were simply appointed by the Jewish community. Some thought that they would be in a better position to negotiate with the Germans. Others believed that they had a better chance to survive and not be subjected to the abuse and harassment, at least to a lesser extent than the population at large.

All the Germans had to do was inform the Judenrat of their demands: jewelry, furs or a certain number of people for 'work'. They knew their demands would be met, or else. The 'obedient' servants would go to work to execute the order of the 'super race representatives'. The Jewish Police would assist the German or the Ukrainian Police to make sure the order was carried out.

Under our new order, things were relatively quiet for a while with a major exception. There was a special elite military unit of the *SS*, called the *Sondercommando,* who would roam about the countryside doing the will of their *Fuehrer.* They would just show up without warning, catch a certain number of Jews who would disappear -- not be heard from again.

Little did we know what was in store for us. None of the Jews believed at the time that, eventually, Hitler would make good on his threats and systematically wipeout an entire people.

Then came December 7, 1941, when the United States was attacked by the Japanese, an ally of Germany. The news came slowly through the radio, the telephone, newspapers (in the bigger towns) and word of mouth. This new development stunned us all. America declared war on Japan and a few days later Germany declared war on the United States. The news may have been slow but the reaction was not.

The day that the United States of America declared war on Germany, the *SS* went on a rampage. The Germans came to Turka with the Ukrainian Police as assistants and caught Jews without warning like a dogcatcher catching dogs. Nearly 500 Jews were put into trucks, taken outside Turka, and lined up on the edge of a long ditch. An *SS* man in white gloves stepped up behind each victim and fired his revolver into each Jew's neck, stepping from victim to victim, an execution military style. Each victim fell into the ditch—the prepared grave, dug by Jews a few hours before. The local population just watched and then eagerly went away to tell the story of the 'spectacle'.

Killings and torture became more frequent. In April 1942, the Ukrainians, with the blessing of the Germans, confiscated all the livestock owned by Jews. We had to deliver our three milk cows to a gathering point where they collected all the cattle to distribute to Ukrainian farmers. So many ironies involved: my poor mother, who gave her blood, sweat and tears for her livestock for over 15 years, now had to give them (not sell them) to those who hated her blindly. Another irony: my mother was so concerned about her cows – little did she know at the time that soon her life would be worth less than her livestock's.

The local population, predominantly Ukrainians, watched from the sides pleased with what they saw; they enjoyed what was happening to the Jews. There was little love between the Jews and the Ukrainians for a number of reasons. First and foremost they considered the Jews to be "Christ killers." More importantly though, they were jealous of Jews who were better educated and economically better off. And in the most blatant prejudice, the Ukrainians, illiterate and suspicious, hated the religious Jews who dressed differently.

It took very little for the Ukrainians to descend upon the hated Jews. That's why when the Germans started the atrocities against the Jews, many Ukrainians and Poles openly robbed and killed countless Jews. Why not? A Gentile killing a Jew was not a criminal offense. The Jews had no one to complain to. Moreover, these murderers didn't consider it wrong to kill Christ killers. Many of them referred to Jews as termites, a term they borrowed from the Germans.

The Jews at this point felt psychologically defeated. There was no hope. They were caught in a web, no where to go, no one to speak to, no one to speak up for the Jews. We knew there was a world out there, but no one cared. The feeling was that there was nothing one could do; just do what you're told, even if it meant going 'willingly to the slaughter' -- just like cattle.

◆   ◆   ◆

Throughout a long and restless night my mind turned over the events that brought us to this point. There had been no news of my family. Dawn was still hours away. All I could do was trust that Uncle Srul and the others who were working to return our people back to the villages would soon bring my family home or bring me news. Did anyone know what was happening, where they were taking all the people from the villages that were not on the list? Where was Uncle Srul?

Srul Hans spent a sleepless night in Turka. He knew that he must do everything to get his wife and daughter released from resettlement to a work camp. His daughter was only 5 years old. There was so much to do. Negotiations begun the day before with the forester Knopf and the Gestapo had not been completed and were to resume later in the morning.

It was still dark. Srul felt something was wrong. There was a hint of dawn so Srul rose and quietly left the house where he had spent the night. Every sense told him that something strange was happening. As he came out into the street, he noticed that the police and the Gestapo were telling every Jew to walk to the railroad station. Soon they started catching Jews in the streets putting them in trucks and transporting them to the railroad station. The Jewish Police were assisting the SS, the German and the Ukrainian Police in the resettlement of the Jews. They had to. Some of the Judenrat as well as the Jewish Police took their jobs very seriously because they thought it was a means of survival. In many cases, if not in most cases, people would do anything to save their own skin at anybody's expense. It was a Darwinian struggle for survival—"better you than me".

Srul's first thought was to get back to the barracks. He noticed that anyone could walk towards the railroad station but not away from it. Even though he was a member of the Judenrat who had freedom of movement, the Germans would not let him walk in that direction. The severity of the problem began to dawn on him very quickly. Something drastic was taking place.

Dawn was about to break but it was still rather dark, when my uncle took off his yellow armband and started to walk in the direction of the barracks, not through the streets but through the fields. In order to get out of the city, Srul had to walk up the hills that surrounded Turka. It wasn't long before a chill passed though his bones, a chill that had nothing to do with the early morning air. The city was surrounded. There were Germans posted about every 100 yards.

Srul knew that the farmers took their cattle out to mountain pastures at a very early hour. As he climbed a hill he could hear cattle moving slowly ahead of the herders. Not having any choice, Srul moved quickly and pretended that he was one of the herders. If any of them was aware of his presence they did not object. Soon, Srul saw that he was out of the city perimeter. He worked his way around until he saw the barracks in the distance without being challenged. Scattered all around the barracks as if a hurricane hit the area were the belongings of the Jews.

Where were the people? Where were his wife and daughter? They must have gone to the station. But why had the Jews left everything scattered about the barracks?

A few days later, I spoke to one of the guys who managed to escape the fate of the cattle cars, and he told me what he saw: throngs of Jews gathered in and around the Russian army barracks in Turka – amongst them, my family. Around them were hundreds of people from nearby villages milling around. The milling stopped as people found resting places and sat on their suitcases or bundles but the hum of fear and a babble of questioning voices came from every direction. The most unnerving sound to everyone was the wailing of the babies and the crying and pleading of the youngest children. Most people sat, accepting, waiting for something to happen and the afternoon dragged on. The word came down that the negotiations regarding the people on the list would resume in the morning.

4

The narrow escape

Gray light crept into our valley ending the black night that threatened to drown my hope. Earlier, only a year or two, when I was truly just a boy, I would have pushed away my fears with that youthful optimism of more innocent times. Too much had happened. I was no longer a boy. Terrible things had forced me toward manhood.

Lying in bed only brought the fears forward. Was my family getting ready to return? Perhaps it was too early. What was happening in Turka? Had the forester Knopf persuaded the Gestapo that the people on the list were valuable and needed for work in the forest? What about Uncle Srul and the Judenrat?

The house was empty, yet full of questions. Dark and still, unlike ordinary days when we would be up and taking care of our livestock, the day was witness to the end of our ordinary lives. It was the quiet that was so unnatural. I wandered about, fears filling my head when I heard the telephone ringing in Markowicz' office. Too early for him to be here, I picked up the receiver.

At first it was just words, a Ukrainian policeman in Turka calling another policeman in an adjacent village. He was full of enthusiasm and satisfaction, "Last night the Gestapo arrived, surrounded Turka, began catching Jews in the street and taking them to the station. Now, they are marching all the Jews in the barracks to the railroad station."

He kept on talking but I didn't hear what he said. My heart froze. I was numb with disbelief. I put down the phone, "No, not my family.

33

They are supposed to be home today." I refused to believe what the Ukrainian said. I rationalized that perhaps my family escaped. They were in the buggy on their way back to Radycz. He wasn't talking about my family. They were on the list. Naively, I believed that those on the list would not be taken away for resettlement.

Time moved with a slowness that pressed the ache in my heart deeper into my being. I welcomed the numbness that suspended me in time. As the sun rose higher over Radycz, word of the German action in Turka came back like hammer blows, each one driving a nail of horror into my mind.

Soon, pieces of the story were hammered into place by people returning from Turka. Little blows of individuals betrayed by their own and bigger blows of the whole misery playing out across the mountains.

The greatest blow came with Uncle Srul's return and his account of the Germans' clearing of the barracks. He came to my house and described the whole situation, but by then it was common knowledge as to what had happened. His wife and daughter, my family, all were taken away.

In some cases, I heard that members of the Judenrat told their own relatives to go to the railroad station. There were things that I could not have done, could not understand, but they had happened. It seemed like a bad story but I learned it was true. The head of the Judenrat in Turka took his own mother to the station. It was more than I could accept. The realization of what had been done to us surged up in a flood of anger.

I knew it now. The whole thing had been a trick—a terrible plot perpetrated by the Germans to fool the Jews, to keep them calm and obedient. The last thing the Germans wanted was a revolt and their plan worked. They were masters at deceit and played to a man's will to survive, a Darwinian survival of the fittest. Those who were willing to do anything to survive did so even if it meant sacrificing their own families.

Around me was the small world into which I had been born 14 years before. The River Stryj, the mountains, our village, our farm, and everywhere I looked, I saw the kind blue eyes of my mother. It was her foresight to ask the head of the village to get me a work permit, that permit with the letter "A" kept me safe on this terrible day.

I knew that the tomorrow of my parents' return would never come. The whole story was brought over the mountains in pieces, carried by many and gathered together into one tale of horror in my mind. August 2nd became known as the "Big Action". In the early light before the real dawn, the *Sonderkommando*, special units of the *SS*, Ukrainian police, and the regular German police had surrounded the entire town of Turka. All the Jews who were inside the barracks were ordered to leave their belongings and march the two miles to the railroad station. Driven before them were Jews caught on the street and snatched from every lane and alley by the club-wielding tormentors. Dragged from their houses, those who hadn't gone to the barracks willingly were forced to join the throngs of frightened Jews who had obeyed the Germans directive.

Several men, who somehow managed to escape, told about the brutality of the march to the station in the broiling sun. The *Sonderkommando,* the police, all the units charged with the delivery of the Jews to the station moved the streams of young and old, men, women, and children along. Those who couldn't keep up were killed on the spot along the road. When the survivors reached the station, they were shoved into waiting cattle cars. The cars had been waiting in the sun and were like ovens. There was no food and more importantly, no water in spite of the scorching heat. Under these inhumane conditions and with no sanitary facilities, what took place that day defies imagination.

The train waited in the station for several hours while the imprisoned Jews sweltered in the heat. Finally, the engine built up steam and slowly pulled away from the station toward Lvov. The Judenrat immediately hired several gentiles to follow the train. They managed to follow it for 50 miles until they reached Lvov, a large city of several hundred thousand. In the city, they lost track of the train and its 4000 Jews, at least three-quarters of the Jewish population of Turka and the surrounding areas.

Lvov, a crossroads where main rail lines fan out over Poland, was a central point for the transport of Jews for resettlement. Now that the true nature of the Germans' plans was known, there was no doubt in my mind that my family and all the people of Turka were destined for one of the major camps along the line. Word came to us that the transport from Turka moved on toward its final destination, the extermination camp at Belzec.

The terrible truth of their fate tore at my heart. I felt that the pain would never go away. The thought of the agony that they must have suffered ate away at my soul. It was beyond my understanding. How is something like this possible?

The realization that my mother was already dead by the time I learned what had happened stiffened my resolve to survive—no, to prevail over this horror. I would do more than survive.

Our village looked as it had before the day of the "Big Action". Radycz seemed unaffected by what was happening all around. We were just one Jewish family of four and now only one of us was left. Many Ukrainians in the village felt bad about the whole tragedy, but there were many more of those who believed that those Jews who didn't accept Christ would perish. The only way to save one's life was to convert to Christianity. Uncle Srul encouraged me to join him and the rest of the few remaining Jews in the adjacent village of Ilnik.

Uncle Srul was right. There was no reason to stay in Radycz except for my mother's last instructions to look after the house. The son of Markowicz, the head of my village, would make sure that no one took anything from the house. When I left, he moved into our house. The whole thing seemed very unreal, very hopeless, very sad, but despite it all, I felt I had to go on. I took a few basics and walked the two miles to Ilnik to join my uncle Srul and Moyshe Hans who were considered the leaders in the Jewish community. Moyshe Hans, was in charge of the Jews who worked in the forest.

Only 40 Jews remained of the 250 in Ilnik and Radycz. There were very few Jewish women left in the village and most of the men worked in the forest cutting timber for the German industry and thus had the "A" work permit. Moyshe and Uncle Srul obtained a labor card for me and I began going to the forest with them. The administrator of the forest operation was Knopf, a folksdeutsch, a term known as not a pure German but of German descent -- nevertheless a German. He was very friendly toward Jews and had tried to negotiate with the Gestapo on the day of the "Big Action" but couldn't help much.

Every day we went into the forest and cut timber hauling it down toward the river. Things seemed quiet as autumn approached. Several weeks after I moved to Ilnik, without warning the German *SS* unexpectedly came to Turka and began catching Jews like animals, throwing them into trucks and hauling them away, not to be seen again. These surprise raids became more and more frequent. We now knew what the Germans planned for the Jews. There was no doubt about it; it was just a matter of time. Thoughts about what action to take began to fill our minds. We wouldn't wait as those who had been taken before had done. Some suggested going to Hungary. It wasn't that far away but several who tried got caught and others may have met death along the way. The risk was too great.

One thing was clear. We couldn't maintain the status quo—it was like waiting for the angel of death. And so every morning, day after day, about 25-30 of us would walk to the forest to work and come back in the in the evening with not only heavy heart, but the fear of the unknown. I felt much safer when my Uncle Srul and Moyshe were around. Unfortunately, they weren't around too often. To play it safe, they would spend time with friendly farmers, especially at night. Although the days were just as fearful, somehow the night was even more threatening. You never knew when or where the next blow was coming.

I recall on several occasions there were secretive talks about escaping to Hungary. I never knew whether or not I was included. Even though Srul was my uncle, there was something distant about the way he treated me. He never made me feel like I was his flesh and blood and he never told me that, no matter what, I shouldn't worry (remember, I was only 14 years old!). The naked truth was that Uncle Srul, if it ever came to it, would save his own life—not mine or anyone else's -- and wouldn't think twice about it. I knew it and I knew something else. I was addicted to life; it was survival at any cost.

Moyshe Hans was a shrewd operator and had a good reputation among farmers. Aware of his powerful position among us, he would take advantage of the situation by making everyone feel that we were dependent on him completely. He was selfish and conceited, but not a fool by any means. Although he had only enough schooling to get by, he had natural intelligence. Moyshe liked to make promises but preferred not to keep them. If he did anything for you, you were indebted to him forever. On a personal note, he was good looking and even before the war I heard stories that he was a big womanizer.

Uncle Srul, on the other hand, although a cousin and a brother-in-law to Moyshe, didn't have the basic intelligence that Moyshe did. He did have quite a following among the farmers, though. He got along very well with them, played cards and socialized with them. This was helpful to him during the difficult times; the local farmers would let no harm come to him.

He was a lumber broker and he did well financially. Always walking around with his hands in his pockets, he would shake them so that everyone could hear the sound of the change jingling. Uncle Srul was a good-natured guy, but very deceptive. He had a permit from Polish authorities to carry a gun and did so. He had his own horse and carriage and he dressed well, not so much for himself but to show off. Seducing women, was one of his main pastimes and he had no problems getting any good-looking woman -- even if she was married. Srul had plenty of time to fool around; he didn't marry until he was 37.

Shadows deepened as the sun rose later each morning and frost greeted us in the early hours when we went into the forest. It was late autumn, October of 1942, and the days were getting chillier. One of the Ilnik men, Isaac Weicher worked in the forester Knopf's office and warned us that the Germans had ordered the revocation of certain labor cards. It wasn't official yet so we still had the vital right to work for a number of days. Not all cards were being revoked but the writing was on the wall. When the order became official, anyone who had his permit revoked would be fair game for the Germans.

One of those revocations was mine.

Time was running out. I had to take action. I had no intention of waiting for the *SS - Sonderkommando* or whomever the Germans would send. Although the order was for us to report to Turka to a labor camp, I knew what that meant and I wasn't going to fall for it. The memory of my family was still raw and I didn't believe anything the Germans said.

I wasn't the only one losing the protection of the labor cards. Mendel Feller, a fellow worker in the forest, and his two brothers, had their permits revoked. Aron Hans, a distant cousin, was in a similar predicament. Mendel Feller was mechanically inclined; a guy with quite an imagination. In fact, there was a joke circulating that Mendel bragged that he could build an airplane and fly us out to safety, a statement that haunted him for a long time.

He was the first one who suggested we build a bunker deep in the forest.

The few of us who knew our labor cards were being revoked were chosen to start building the bunker. We had to move fast, winter was closing in on us. And so, for the next few days instead of going to work to cut timber, a group including my uncle Srul and Moyshe searched for a place to build the bunker. As a foreman, Moyshe had leeway in accounting for their time. They would have to look for just the right location. Mendel figured that the bunker had to be located deep in the woods and far from the village. It had to be not easily accessible, inconspicuous, reasonably close to water, and, a place that could give us room to escape if we were ever attacked; not an easy task.

After a few days of walking and searching, we found such a place in a part of the forest called Rostoka. Everyday for about two weeks, those of us whose labor cards were being revoked, would start out from the village as if we were going to work cutting timber. Instead we picked up axes, shovels, and other necessary equipment, and went deep in the forest to build our bunker. Mendel Feller, the bunker designer and supervisor, spoke with authority and was eager to get the job done. Rivka, his wife, who somehow had managed to escape transport with the other Jewish women, was with him. Mendel was very devoted to his wife, but he had to have the final word.

Aron Hans, another of our bunker-builders was a bachelor at 35. He was easy going, but when pushed too far he would get extremely irritated and show it. He always let someone else make the big decisions.

There was another Mendel in our group, Mendel Fuchs, about 50, who had lost his wife in the Big Action of August 2nd. They never had any children. Mendel Fuchs was not too literate and had a bad reputation. He used to deal with cattle, and was able to put it over on farmers through trickery, lots of verbosity and a very thick accent. A good 'actor', he enjoyed feeling sorry for himself and liked it when others did the work.

Strange what you remember about people. There was one man in our group that I remember because he would cry on high holy days. It used to leave an insecure impression seeing a man at that age with tears rolling down his cheeks. Leibish Abel, a man slightly over 50, had lost his wife and 6 children in the Big Action. Before the turmoil of the war he dealt with small and large cattle, and struggled to make ends meet. Leibish was a good storyteller.

I wasn't the only young man working on the bunker. Shaye Schwartz was about my age, around 15. His work number was also up. He lost his whole family the same way I did. His father was a shoemaker and their large family was very poor. (Shaye had extremely flat feet and walked in a rather peculiar way.) He was insecure and didn't stand up for himself. Everyone took advantage of him, especially the older guys, as if they inherited the right to push him around.

David Berg was in the Polish Army. During the war, a bullet hit his middle finger of his right hand, and because he didn't have it fixed, it curled in. When you shook hands with him you couldn't help but feel the finger in your palm. He was physically strong; he was a "doer". David, a man of strong convictions, was fair, but even if he was wrong, which happened on occasion, he was right. You could never convince him that there was another way to look at things—David Berg was stubborn.

In Ilnik, my uncle Moyshe-Avrum Hans hadn't been required to report during the Big Action because he had a labor card. A man of about 55 years, he, unfortunately, was in bad health. His wife had died in the August 2nd transport to Belzec. Through the autumn, he became progressively worse until one day in November he died in his brother Srul's arms. Normally, we would have taken him to Turka to the big Jewish cemetery for burial, but these were not normal times. Uncle Srul found a quiet place outside the village on the side of a hill. We couldn't leave any sign for fear that the wrong people would find the grave.

When I moved to Ilnik, I lived in my uncle Moyshe-Avrum's house, which was only about 50 feet away from Moyshe Hans' house. After the Big Action most of the remaining 50 Jews in Ilnik had moved into five houses for consolidation. They felt it was better to stick together and better for security reasons, even though by then the Ukrainians didn't bother us that much.

The Ukrainians began to realize that the Germans and Hitler weren't the answer to their problems of nationalism; besides the war began to take a turn for the worse for the Germans. Those whose behavior was nothing to be proud of when the war broke out began to worry about the future.

Each house had three rooms, enough space to accommodate about 15 people. Moyshe Hans's house was unoccupied and most of the group of people stayed in my deceased uncle's house. There were a few women around, who, for whatever reasons, didn't obey the order to go the barracks like all the "good citizens". Two or three of the women cooked for some of the men. People lived from day to day knowing their days were numbered, just not knowing when and where. I never had any doubts that I would survive. I had the feeling that my mother kept an eye on me and I knew, even if it seemed irrational, that I would make it.

We lived for news. The search for it occupied much of our time. Even if it was phony, untrue or a downright lie, we liked to hear it and tell and retell the news again and again. We had various sources of news. First, there was the newspaper, which was a very rare commodity. Then there were farmers. The more sophisticated ones came from Turka where they had occasion to talk to the "intelligencia" who presumably had "reliable" information from "unquestionable" sources. And then there was "us"—the gifted ones would hear a word and were able to make a story out of it; exaggerating the truth was a very strong psychological factor that helped not only cheer us up but keep us alive. Last but not least, there was simply putting your ear to the ground and listening to the earth. You could hear pounding which sounded like heavy guns. I did this a number of times and it definitely picked up my spirits. Whether the noise I heard was gunfire or something else wasn't important, the important thing was that someone was fighting the Germans and it was good to hear.

The weather was exceptionally good and so day after day we dug into the mountain to build our bunker. We wanted to make the bunker as difficult as possible to detect, even from close by. The place that we chose was secluded. The side of the mountain plunged down toward a wooded valley and it was the steep angle that would assure that our bunker was easily overlooked. We hacked and dug straight into the side of the mountain. We leveled the floor as we worked, cutting a wedge into the mountain. As we dug into the soil and moved rocks and boulders, we began to form a low wall of earth, rock and logs across the front of the deepening excavation. When we were all through, logs and brush would form a roof slanting down from the topmost part of the dig to the low wall in the front. Then our wedge chopped into the mountain, covered with brush and leaves, would look like the undisturbed side of the mountain wall making a snug and secret hideout in the forest.

Mendel Feller was proud of his and our accomplishments. We had been working on the bunker for about two weeks, and with each passing day, the weather got cooler. Winter, in our part of the country, starts in early November and lasts until about the beginning of May. Snow began to fall, lightly at first. Our group's mood got gloomier and gloomier, particularly since we were facing a long winter and time was running out. We felt helpless and hopeless, like being caught in a web, like frozen panic. In spite of all this we had a strong will to live, to survive.

The pressure on us mounted with each day as it got colder and colder. By now, the bunker was in fairly good shape except for our cooking requirements. We needed a stove and some utensils. What we were really after wasn't a stove in the conventional way; it was just the flat metal surface that we could put on top of two rows of rocks for support. With a fire under the metal sheet we could cook—like a barbeque. Almost every house in the village had such a metal sheet.

Mendel Feller and I decided to get such a metal sheet from the stove of one the houses. Since no one had lived in Moyshe Hans' house since the Big Action, we took that one. After work, we went down into Ilnik leaving behind Aron Hans, Mendel Fuchs and Leibish Abel, who had already moved into the bunker.

It was November 17th. I will never forget that date. That evening, when we got to the village, there were rumors that some farmers, who just arrived from Turka, were talking about some activities going on. The rumors said that the Gestapo had arrived and they were going into the villages to round up Jews. Mendel Feller and I and those who no longer had labor cards, decided to leave the village and go to the bunker.

Since we were extremely hungry and the cooking smelled so good, we decided to eat first. As soon as we ate, Mendel and I went next door to Moyshe Hans' deserted house, which was about fifty feet away. Our intention was to grab the metal plate off the stove and disappear in a hurry.

The night was cold and clear, a bright moon—almost full, reflected off three inches of snow covering the ground. To us, who would rather not be noticed, it seemed like daylight. We let ourselves into Uncle Moyshe's house. It was dark and difficult to see after the brightness of the moon. I lit a candle. We looked around for some utensils and I held the candle while Mendel took the metal plate off the stove.

Shielding the candle to hide the light as I was near a window, I looked out and saw a German policeman, gun out and running toward the house. I shouted, "Police;" the candle fell from my hand. I ran.

Dashing through two rooms of Moyshe's long house, I ran into a third room. My chances of escaping alive were next to nil but I ran as fast as I could heading for a window and a chance.

As I jumped out of the window, a man caught my hand. In a calm Polish voice, he reassured me that nothing will happen to me and I should just calm down. He was dressed like civilian and I immediately recognized that he was a Jewish policeman when I saw his armband. I was stunned. The shock of being caught, of what was happening to me made me all the more determined to survive. I knew that I had to get out. I will not go with them. Wherever they are going to take me, I will not go with them.

The German policeman joined my Jewish captor and led me toward Moyshe-Avrum's house. I remembered stories I had heard about what happened when the Germans caught a Jew. It didn't matter what the Jew had done, disobeyed an order, made a mistake or nothing at all except be a Jew. The Germans would take their captive to the cemetery or stand him against a wall anywhere facing the policeman who would then shoot and kill him. To me this was horrible, dreadful and unthinkable. I vowed that I would never get in that situation. I will run. I won't face a bullet. They will have to shoot me in the back—some choice. Now, I was about to make that choice.

The three of us walked toward the house where Mendel and I had just eaten a welcome supper with the other Jews who were still inside. Did they know what was happening?

As we were about to enter the house, the policemen told me to lie down outside on the snowy ground. They caught two more guys outside the house and told them to lie down on the ground. The German policeman stood over us with his rifle ready. Within seconds I began lifting my head very slowly, as inconspicuously as possible, to see what was happening. Could I escape? With the German standing over me, it was unrealistic, even silly to think of escaping. He saw my movement and stepped toward me and drove his heavy boot into my chest. I passed out. I recovered, gasping for breath, my chest permanently dented from the blow. I still have the scar to this day.

I lay on the snow trying to recover my senses and get my breath. In a few minutes, the policemen ordered us to get up and go into the house. Inside I saw two more Germans and two more Jewish policemen.

In the first room, all the Jews were getting dressed. Through the kitchen there was another room where others were dressing. I was surprised to see that the kitchen between the rooms was dark. In it was the bed where my uncle Moyshe-Avrum had died a few weeks before. A thought flashed in my head. I will hide under the bed. When they take everyone out, they won't miss me right away. I will run into the forest and escape. I had to work fast. There was firewood for the stove stored under the bed. Desperate to escape, I grabbed wood pushing it aside to make room. One, two, three pieces of wood moved toward the back. I pushed more away and crawled into the opening to make more room. As I wedged myself farther under the old bed I needed only another foot of space to squeeze my body under and tuck my legs out of sight. I reached for another log and pushed.

I didn't hear the German policeman come into the room. Pain shot through my legs. Something crashed down on them. One of the Germans shouted at me as he struck my legs and ordered me into the other room to sit on the floor. The Jewish policeman saw what was happening and asked me how old I was.

"I am seventeen," I answered. It was better to be older if selected for work.

The Jewish policeman muttered in Polish to himself, "*Szkoda takiego chlopaka,*" pity such a young boy. Then he asked, "Do you have any money or valuables?"

I realized exactly what he meant. If I had money I could buy myself out. I said, "No". But I did have ten zlotys, equivalent to about two dollars, perhaps. I didn't want to lose any opportunity, so I approached him and said, "I am young and I have a good chance to survive. I can give you ten zlotys".

He smiled sarcastically as if he controlled the entire universe. "I get thousands for this."

"I realize," I said, "but I don't have it."

One of the German policemen approached me. "How many Jews live here?"

I wanted to give him an honest answer and started counting how many Jews lived in each room. They were moving about from room to room too much for me to count any other way but I must have taken too much time. The German started hitting me in the face again and again. Blood ran from my nose. I could taste it in the back of my mouth.

The same Jewish policeman, the one I was negotiating with, intervened and said to the German "I will ask him". He turned to me and said in a very stern voice, "I am going to ask you but you better tell me the truth or else".

"I will, I will," I answered realizing immediately that honesty was not important, any reasonable number would do. He gave a few minutes to take care of my bloody nose. "Fourteen," I said and that ended that.

There was commotion everywhere. People were getting dressed or looking for things. The atmosphere was unreal, unbelievable. I know they all felt the same as I. A rope was tightening around everyone's neck—the end has come. It is like seeing the angel of death manifest in the form of a policeman. No one among us spoke. Except for the rustle of everyone getting ready to go, it was quiet. We were living a nightmare. It could not be real, but it was and yet I refused to believe it. Somehow, at least in me, there was a spark of hope.

I pretended to look for things, all the while my mind raced through the possibilities, the ideas of escape, running away, or somehow just disappearing. I was desperate because my immediate chances were poor. I couldn't see myself leaving this house with the rest of the group. One thought ran over and over in my mind, *I must get out of this mess.*

Instinctively, I went over to the Jewish policeman who had asked me if I had money. I appealed to him again. This time he did not reject it outright, but gave it a second thought. I saw immediately, not convincingly, a ray of hope.

"How much money do you have?" he asked.

"Ten zlotys."

"Give the money," he said and went over to the German policeman. He whispered something to him and then came back to me. "Go over and thank the German."

I did as I was told even though it might have been the same German that gave me a bloody nose. The German policeman then told me to stay in the house. After everyone leaves, I must stay until the authorities arrive, watching the house and the property inside to make sure no one takes anything. I agreed.

As soon as everyone left I found my jacket and hat, which I had left under the bed. I had no intention of staying in the house any longer then I had to and hoped that they didn't change their minds while I was still there. Taking a loaf of bread, I too left the house but from the opposite side.

The side of the building where I walked out led to the main road. On that main road, stood a Jewish policeman, presumably in charge of something. Of one thing I was sure, he had no gun—but physically I would have been no match for him. As I was leaving, the Jewish policeman said, "Hold, where are you going" in German. I answered in German saying they let me out. I assumed he understood what had taken place, most likely a payoff and so he said to me "go to the devil". I could not understand why he would make this kind of a statement, but it sounded beautiful to me. I wasted no time and walked quietly but briskly. About 50 yards down the road, I heard noises coming from the direction I just left. By then no bullet could catch me. I scrammed among the farmers' huts to a side road outside the village and toward the mountain.

5

The Bunker in Rostoka

Snow crunched under my feet sounding ten times as loud as I knew it could. The sky was still clear and I had no trouble seeing where I was going in the bright moonlight. Unfortunately, this revealed my presence to anyone around and I feared that I would be stopped. "I mustn't run. Just keep walking toward the main road" I thought to myself. I was almost outside the main road, and ready to turn left to go towards the mountain, when I met one of the farmers that I knew. He must have seen that I was frightened and suggested that I calm down. After assuring me that there was no danger, he told me that my uncle Srul and Moyshe had gone up the mountain. I was very happy to hear the news because that was exactly where I was headed. Up to now I felt that everyone else was gone and I was the only one remaining.

I started to run in that direction. About 15 minutes later, I saw two men silhouetted against the moon-bright snow. I thought they must be Srul and Moyshe but I wasn't sure. As I got closer, all doubt left and I started to yell for them to slow down. They motioned to me not to yell, but somehow I didn't have the same fear they did. I knew what was happening in the village. They didn't, not completely. When I finally caught up with them, they told me that they had been on their way to Moyshe-Avrum's house where we had been staying but met a farmer walking in the opposite direction. He knew what was happening and told Srul and Moyshe to turn back. They said that an angel must have sent him when the farmer told them, "Don't go there." For a moment the two hesitated, but the farmer grabbed them by the shoulders and physically turned them back. He then told them to disappear and this is how they wound up going up the mountain.

Being with Srul and Moyshe gave me an added sense of security; and I was so happy to have caught up with them. In my eyes, being young as I was, I thought if I stick with them or if they stick with me, my chances of survival were much better. There were times I worried that they would just vanish. The two would stick together like glue. They had a good relationship with the farmers, better than anyone among us. That put Moyshe and Srul in an enviable position in the eyes of the remaining Jews who looked up to them for that reason.

I was on the hill overlooking the horror I had just experienced. Moyshe, Srul and I began to discuss where we should go. The bunker? If not, where? The bunker might be too dangerous. I thought this was the reason we built the bunker. Why ask where to go? We built the bunker to hide in the forest and now we were going to find another place to hide. The main reason we were reluctant to go back to the bunker was that if the Germans had caught some of us they might pressure them to spill the beans. A day or two with the Gestapo or the German Police might get it out of those who knew. Then the Germans would catch us all. We decided not to go back to the bunker.

What other choice did we have? We could've asked one of the farmers to hide us, but let's face it, we were fugitives from justice -- German "justice" – and condemned to die nevertheless. Any farmer we approached for sanctuary was risking his life. Kill the Jews and kill those who help them. There was also the problem of discovery and betrayal for the reward—cigarettes, alcohol, sugar, anything scarce could be traded for a Jew. Whether it was the bunker or possibly a farmer, we were on the wrong side of the village, which we had to cross at some point. More importantly, we had to cross the river to get to the other side. Crossing the village and the river were extremely dangerous; the water was cold, the moon was full on the brilliant snow, and it was freezing cold. We could be seen for miles. Of course, we had no choice; we had to do it.

The river was shallow, only about 2 to 3 feet deep, but very wide, two long city blocks or perhaps wider. As frightened as I was, I knew that I could do almost anything. We chose a sparsely populated spot, took off our shoes and waded into the river. The frigid water made my legs go numb long before we reached the other side but I forced them to move one step at a time. It seemed like hours and as I staggered up the bank on the other side I was sure I would never recover. I suppose there are certain body defenses that take over and ward off colds, pneumonia or any other kind of disease. Standing wet and exhausted on the dry land I wondered if I would sicken before the dawn. A warm fire, hot food and blankets would have been welcome but all I had was a loaf of bread. The three of us shared a piece. We still had to decide where to go.

Moyshe and Srul decided to go to the forester whom they knew, by the name of Joseph Markowicz. The forester also knew my family and me but Moyshe told me to go to a neighbor and not to overwhelm the forester. I wasn't pleased with his decision but I wasn't going to argue. I knew Srul wouldn't back me.

I went to my immediate neighbor, Nikolay Markowicz. The two Markowiczes weren't related (many villagers had the same last name). Because my mother had given our neighbor clothing and other things for safekeeping at times, I felt I could go there for help.

When I appeared at their door, miraculously they let me in. I suspected they were apprehensive about letting me stay, knowing that the penalty for hiding a Jew was death. I was well aware of that and, as desperate as I was, after staying there for two days I decided to go to the bunker in Rostoka. After all, that's what the bunker was built for and besides, there was no other place for me to go.

When I arrived at the bunker I met the rest of the gang. David Berg and Aron Hans were glad to see that I had escaped and told me what they knew about others from Ilnik. They informed me that three sisters, whose parents were taken away in The Big Action, might join our group. The three Rosenberg sisters were being hidden at a farmer's house in Ilnik -- Feige, Elke and Blime Rosenberg, were 20, 18, and 16. Feige and Elke were taken away together with the other people on the night I was caught, November 17, 1942, but from a different location in the village. I found out that it had been a coordinated raid by the German and Ukrainian Police assisted by the Jewish Police. Feige jumped from the train on the way from Turka to the Sambor ghetto. Somehow she squeezed through a narrow opening in the cattle car, as the train slowed down approaching a bend. Elke walked back to Ilnik after being released in Sambor by a strange coincidence. Being a young woman, who spoke Ukrainian fluently without an accent, it was much easier for her to be mistaken for a gentile. A man didn't have that privilege, either because of the accent but more importantly because of circumcision. Blime was working for a farmer in another village. At any rate, after some discussion, we all decided to have the girls join us, even though no one was interested in getting involved in a relationship. It was difficult enough to take care of oneself, in more than one way, without getting involved with another person particularly someone of the opposite sex. That could be difficult.

After a few days the girls joined us in the bunker. Our bunker was high up in the hill that overlooked the valley. The location was a good one to detect if someone was coming to get us. There was water not too far away, which played a major part in the choice of location when the bunker was in the planning stages. Now that we were entering the coldest stage of winter, we knew that the biggest threat to our existence was the snow. Snow means tracks. The less we walked around the fewer tracks we revealed. We would have to severely restrict our movements. Fire would have to be limited to a few hours, and never in daytime—the smoke would give us away. We had some food in the bunker, a few days' supply, but certainly not enough to keep us going for a long time.

Each time we left the bunker we risked detection. We had to go down to the village every few days to get food, and more importantly, we had to find out if anyone knew about us (rumor or otherwise). Even a rumor was enough to die a thousand times. This was all new to us. We were surrounded. There were enemies real and imaginary on all sides. Everyone in the bunker was numb at this point. We were all sitting ducks and we didn't know how to function or what to expect. Outside the bunker, the terrain was white with snow; even the trees didn't provide us with much protection.

News came to us in the bunker in scraps and pieces picked up from farmers when we went into the village to replenish our food supplies. When I moved to the bunker I was surprised to see Mendel Feller there. I had known that his wife Rivka had been there some time but the last time I had seen Mendel was the night we went to take the metal plate for the bunker stove and got caught.

Mendel told me that when the police caught me jumping out of the window, they assumed that there was someone else with me. He saw what happened to me and he decided to hide inside a closet. I told Mendel what had happened to me and how all the Jews living in the house had been taken away. He said that while we were all getting dressed in the adjacent house, a German policeman and two Jewish policemen were searching for him. They were almost ready to give up the search when Mendel heard a Jewish policeman say, "Let's take a look in the closet," and that's exactly where he was.

By this time I had offered my tiny but successful bribe and left for the mountain but Mendel was taken to the group and they all walked to a gathering point down in the village. There they met other groups gathered in similar operations in three different locations in the village. Mendel told me that the Jews and the policemen went by horse and carriage to Turka. Then they were loaded into cattle cars and taken by train about 40 miles away to the Sambor ghetto, but Mendel wasn't with them.

After the police caught Mendel, he realized that if he didn't escape some way then and there, he might not ever get another chance. With his wife Rivka already in the bunker he had good reason to want to get away. He went to a Jewish policeman to make a deal. The policeman then spoke to a German. Mendel had something I didn't have, a valuable article to bargain with.

Mendel offered him a gold watch, a very rare commodity. The German wanted the gold watch. Mendel told them that the watch was hidden at one of the farmer's houses. The three of them (the German, a Jewish policeman and Mendel) went to get the watch. While they were gone, another German and a Jewish policeman went to pick up some more Jews that lived close by, leaving the rest of the Jews unattended. They had at least half an hour to escape, but much to his surprise, and mine, no one left. The only exception was Shaye Schwartz, a boy of about 15 who just got "lost" while they were marching.

The German got his watch and Mendel got out of his mess.

We had all been rounded up in the action of November 17, 1942. But in a few short weeks, the Germans had issued instructions that the entire area was to be cleansed of Jews. The "magic" day, December 1, 1942, was called Judenfrei, which meant "free of Jews". After that day, no Jew was supposed to exist in any shape or form, alive in the area. The only place a Jew could go was to the Sambor Ghetto, a place for future slaughtering. Incidentally, the Jews that decided to report to the Germans rather than hide, were, instead of being sent to the ghetto, taken to the cemetery and killed facing the executioners, a sight I couldn't bear to imagine.

We subsequently heard from farmers that there were a few stragglers from other villages who were on their way to report to the German authorities in accordance with the instructions regarding Judenfrei. I could not understand why anyone would listen to the Germans, especially at this point, and believe what they were saying about the transfer to a labor camp. On the other hand, I could sympathize with those who were reporting. They were tired; had lost hope for anything; lost the drive to fight for survival. The weather was cold and snowy; their relations with the farmers were cool at best. The farmers were not willing to take a chance because their own lives were at risk. If caught, the farmer faced the same penalty as a Jew. The only solution left for those hopeless people was to go to the Sambor ghetto—a horribly terrifying thought.

Several days passed. Moyshe went down to the village of Ilnik. When he returned shortly before dawn, he said that he had been told that there was a strong possibility that a forester by the name of Metzger who was in the area had either seen the bunker or tracks in the snow. It was somewhat vague but enough to scare the hell out of us.

A decision had to be made and made in a hurry. The question haunted us. What to do? Where to go? One answer was clear—we couldn't stay where we were; we just couldn't take the chance.

6

The Bunker at Opolonik

While staying at the forester Joseph Markowicz' place after November 17, Moyshe and Srul told him about the difficulties of hiding in the forest, especially the risk of detection when winter snows covered the area. Markowicz suggested that if we ran into a difficult situation, we could move into the part of the forest that was under his control, so to speak. The time had come to take him up on his suggestion. It was risky to entrust our lives to one man, but what choice did we have? After discussing the pros and cons, the group came to the conclusion that we had to take that chance. We didn't waste any time; each one of us gathered together our belongings, meager though they were. The little we had saved or collected comprised a person's entire "wealth".

Early in the morning our little group left the diminishing safety of our bunker and we picked our way through heavy snow, our breath freezing in suspension on the cold mountain air. The forest was still dark and quiet. Tall fir trees shrouded in snow and frost standing sentinel over our trail, our footsteps crunching in the crusty snow were the only sounds to disturb any living creature. Our march to Markowicz' part of the forest called Opolonik (pronounced "op-o-LO-nik"), which was near my village of Radycz was over 25 miles.

The entire area was part of the Carpathian mountain ridge with its variety of mountains and deep forests. Needless to say, the 15 of us walking in one line left quite a trail in the snow. We had to do something about that. David Berg came up with an idea to hide any trace of our passage. We would take a branch from a tree and drag it along behind us. Everyone took turns; the last person on line dragged the branch behind him, erasing the telltale path.

By late afternoon we arrived at our new destination. Fortunately, the snow was not too deep in spots, which helped to cut down our walking time, a period when we were most vulnerable to discovery. The same question had come up again, "exactly where do we settle down?" It must not be too accessible and it must be close to the water, and not too conspicuous.

As dangerous as it was, we had to go into the village to get food, which was, as always, scarce. No matter who brought in the food, our chef Mr. Mendel Feller, who was in charge of our central "kitchen", prepared it. When the food was ready to eat, Mendel would dole it out to each of us. Everyone would look and watch. God forbid one person should get a drop more. Some of us grew resentful and placed a special watch when Mendel handed over the plate of food to his wife or his brothers. When you live in such close quarters, nerves fray and little things take on an unreasonable importance. Mendel created much of the resentment towards himself especially as he seemed to control our life-sustaining food supply. Many in our group couldn't forget his constant bragging about how he would build an airplane and fly us all out. Now that we were trapped in our mountains in constant peril, they teased him about his promised plane that would never come. This teasing brought us all temporary relief.

The bunker was small. We were beginning to settle in; getting used to the fear of the known and the unknown. Going to the village was a problem. We were all very concerned about the trail we left in the snow. I had the feeling we were caught in a web and a maze, trapped with no way to get free.

Moyshe and I went down to the village to see my immediate neighbor, Nikolay Markowicz. He had a very good relationship with my family and it was with him that I spent the two days after my escape. Markowicz, no relation to Joseph Markowicz, owned two oxen, which he used on his farm for everything, plowing, hauling manure, transporting wood for heating, and delivering lumber to Turka. He was not a rich man. Like the rest of the farmers he used his earned money to purchase salt, sugar and other basic necessities for the farm.

Moyshe and I told him about our concern over the tracks we left in the snow every time anyone left the bunker to go down into the village. He understood our problem and we were able to persuade him to take his oxen and sleds up to the forest and to erase the trail at least once a week. This was an enormous favor to us but also a great risk. He knew our location, exactly.

Since one of us would always stand guard outside the bunker, we arranged for some kind of signal to let us know that it was Nikolay and not anyone else. Nikolay told us that when he would pass in the vicinity of the bunker, he would yell out as if he was yelling at the oxen to move faster. This had a very calming effect on us.

The environment was never foreign to us; after all, this is where we grew up. But, at the same time, it was completely different. Outside the bunker, we could see nothing but snow, the trees, an occasional bird or rabbit. It was quiet, serene; it felt almost like the Garden of Eden, and yet not one of us knew whether this would be their last day. It seemed we were far from civilization, embraced by the "safety" of the environment, until there was a knock on the tree by a bird or a distant crack by an animal on the move. Suddenly our antennas would go up. Who is it? What is it? Is it something serious?...it could be...maybe not? We gained the instincts of wild animals, alert and ready to flee.

In the bunker, Moyshe, Srul, and Aron passed the time playing cards. Leibish, the man who would cry while praying, was grateful for any help but content if you left him alone. Pleased if you paid attention and talked to him, he liked to tell stories as long as you listened to him. Like most groups of people thrown together in dire circumstances, we had our hard workers and a few who did as little as possible. One of the latter was Mendel Fuchs, a businessman who often schemed how to get something for nothing and get away with it. He would complain that he didn't feel well, especially if there was something he was supposed to do. On one occasion, Moyshe and another person brought food from the village in heavy rucksacks. After carrying their burdens so far they decided to leave the two bags at the bottom of the hill and have someone from the bunker pick them up. All of a sudden Mendel Fuchs said he had a severe backache; no one was buying his story. It was his turn to go down and pick up the bags—which he did.

Isolated as we were, there was, believe it or not, an opportunity for romance. Having three young women living in such close quarters, it didn't take long for one of our young men to catch the eye of one of them. David Berg had his eye on Elke Rosenberg. Even though, under the circumstances, it was preferable to be alone and not get involved with anybody as far as I was concerned, I saw that he had strong feelings for her.

Winter pressed its snowy hand on our mountains making life difficult and dangerous. We tried not to wander too far from the bunker and always feared that our tracks would lead the wrong people to our hideout. Each trip down to the village was a risk that had to be taken and we were grateful for my neighbor's help. Nikolay Markowicz kept his word and came with his oxen and sleds to erase the tracks in the snow. He would pass by the area and give us the usual signal. We knew it was Nikolay and welcomed his holler.

Even though the forester Joseph Markowicz was on our side, we still had apprehensions about being so close to the village. But, we trusted him; what choice did we have? The fact that Nikolay Markowicz came around with his oxen almost weekly, especially after a snowfall, gave us some sense of safety. There was always that nagging doubt, but we were fortunate; our trust was never betrayed.

All sorts of thoughts would go through my mind. The constant "what ifs" plagued me with doubts. The Germans offered very exciting rewards of tobacco, alcohol and other scarce luxuries for catching, informing, and delivering Jews to the authorities. I was well aware of the enticements dangled before poor and ignorant farmers. In another village where the Ukrainians hated the Jews as much as the Germans, we wouldn't have lasted a week. But here we were among friends.

In mid-February 1943, we were in our new bunker for about a month when one day, while I was standing guard, Nikolay Markowicz passed by with his oxen and gave the usual holler. I mistook his holler for something sinister. In my mind the voice I heard was that of the Germans looking for us—the worst possible situation. Immediately, I alerted everyone in the bunker without saying specifically what it was. My warning was enough to have everyone out of the bunker in seconds, scattering in different directions. After running for a while, I stopped and tried to figure out what to do next. This happened around noontime, which is when Markowicz would usually pass by with his oxen.

Everyone waited for about two hours, each in a different part of the area. It was very quiet. We began to realize that it was a false alarm. I felt bad and foolish, but glad that nothing had happened. Slowly we gathered around and returned to the bunker. I faced the group confident that it was better to have a false alarm than ignore instincts that might save our lives.

When you live as close to the land as we did in our villages, you learn the little signs of changing seasons that city dwellers might ignore. I had walked these mountains so often to and from Turka and now saw the indications that spring was coming. The days were growing longer; the sunrays were noticeably warmer. As pleasant a thought as that was, it also brought new worries. The snow will begin to melt. The farmers will start to look for hay left in the field in the late fall. Chances of being detected grew much greater.

Although it was getting closer to the Easter holidays, the weather was still very cold particularly at night, which kept the snow from melting. Mornings were crisp and cold. The forest was quiet and the air so still that any voice, however soft, even a whisper, could be heard for miles. The sound of a voice, no matter how far, felt like it was right next to you. On this particular Sunday morning, the people from one village were going to church in an adjacent village. The churchgoers were passing by the edge of the forest where we stayed. Their voices and the noise carried far; it sounded to us like there was some kind of a commotion going on at the edge of the forest. We had to find out what was going on in order to give the group a chance to escape, just in case.

Mendel Feller, Aron Hans and I decided to go and investigate. We came out of the bunker and crossed over into the road used by Markowicz and his oxen. Down the hill we went as quietly as we could. As we approached the edge of the forest, we heard indistinct voices that felt like they were right on top of us. The three of us panicked; in my mind I felt that this was it. We ran back up the hill to notify the others that whatever it was, it was here and imminently threatening.

As we reached the place to turn in toward the bunker, Aron Hans and I were so sure that the Germans and company had come to get us that we decided to go in the opposite direction, into a different mountain wall of the forest. Mendel Feller went to the bunker—his wife was there. Everyone was for himself; it was a question of saving one's life at any cost. Aron Hans and I walked around aimlessly listening for any unusual voices or noises. By then, thank God, everything was quiet. Much later in the afternoon we came back to the bunker and so did everyone else. It was a happy ending although some of the people in the group were not too pleased with our behavior. But then again, they probably would have done the same thing.

One afternoon, at the end of March or the beginning of April 1943, we were all in the bunker when we heard someone knocking at the bunker entrance. It was a knock we had never heard before. Who is on guard? No one knew. Everyone went pale and was just about to die. The "door" opened and in walked Avrum Heger. Heger, a distant cousin of my uncle Srul, owned a liquor store in Turka before the war. He had lost his family in the Big Action the same way as everyone else had. We were pleased to see him, in a way, but at the same time suspicious. How did he get to us? Who told him about us? Who else knows about us? Are we exposed to half of the world? My mind was full of questions and fears. Did anyone follow him? Everyone must have thought the same thing; there were lots of questions, but very few answers. Heger's arrival frightened us, but after a while we calmed down a bit.

Heger said that he was hiding at a farmer's place. The farmer became scared. He suspected that someone who knows about Heger would get him in trouble. Or someone might know someone who believed he knew about Heger. That was the way everyone thought. If there was any reason to believe that there was even a possibility that someone else knows, the penalty for hiding a Jew was the same as being a Jew. Somehow, the farmer found out that there were Jews hiding in the forest, in this particular forest. The farmer, however, wouldn't just let Heger go and wash his hands of the whole matter. He decided to do some investigation and told Heger where to go and how to reach us. His directions were fairly accurate as it turned out (adding to our fears). Heger made a smart decision to look for us in daylight. At night, it probably would've aroused a great deal of suspicion and would've been much more difficult to find us. We were very concerned. If he found us, anybody should be able to find us. In fact, he felt we were so unsafe, Heger went back to the same farmer and told him this was not for him.

The weather was getting warmer and the snow was beginning to melt slowly. Different kinds of problems now confronted us. As we had thought, local farmers were coming out to the fields as they did every spring. Some looking for hay, some for lumber, others to examine the fields soon to be worked. In general, there was more activity all around us. It was now more dangerous to stay in the bunker. We risked discovery and the consequences that would follow. A few of us went down to the village where we were told that we had been spotted.

We decided that we had to abandon the bunker.

Now where do we go? The days might be much warmer, but the nights were very cold. We decided to split up for a few days to wait and see if anyone will go looking for us. Most of us had connections with farmers where we could get food, but to ask to stay over was another story. It was just too risky.

I decided to go to another neighbor, a widow who was fairly friendly with my family. Her name was Yohana. Perhaps, she would let me stay for a few days. I took the chance. I had not seen her since I lost my family. I figured a widow would be more amenable to help me out and not worry that much. She was about 35 and had been a widow for several years. My hunch was right.

At first she was hesitant but then she decided to put me up in the stable where she had two cows, a horse and chickens. I could sleep in the hay. I was very relieved that she agreed to let me stay. After a long winter, I was exhausted, undernourished, weak and always fearful of what might happen. She brought me food. God knew how I needed it.

One day in the hay, one thing led to another and we started to fool around but I couldn't get an erection. For a 15 year-old guy that was unusual and for me it was very frustrating. A year or two earlier I walked around constantly aroused in spite of all our problems. Deep inside I thought that if I could perform, perhaps I could stay there longer. Yohana must have had the same idea and began to restore my health. She fed me well and after five days my problem was solved. While I was pleased about that, I was also hiding in the hay like I was on pins and needles. Being in Radycz, my own village, I felt surrounded from all sides. I could peek out because the stable was located next to the road and I could see people I knew walking on the road talking and going about their lives as if nothing was wrong. If some of them knew how close I was…. All sorts of thoughts went through my mind. I pictured the worst.

It wasn't possible for our entire group to hide with farmers in Radycz because some were from distant villages and didn't know any of the local people. Mendel Fuchs, Mendel Feller and his wife and two brothers along with Shaye Schwarz decided to go to another part of the forest with a steep mountain wall, not easily accessible. It was in Plishka forest and close to where we built our original bunker in Rostoka forest.

Moyshe and Srul decided not to join the group but stay by themselves for a while. I think it's because they felt they had a better chance to survive without the group, and, if necessary, go to another farmer and stay over a few days. I figured out where they were staying and went to join them. Naturally I was glad to be with them. Somehow I felt more secure staying with Moyshe and Srul.

7

The tents of Plishka forest

There was a small area of land with very dense trees surrounded by farmland close to my family's house in Radycz. We thought it was not a conspicuous area and it was close to a little stream. Moyshe, Srul and I decided it would be safe to stay there, at least for the time being.

Moyshe, as a rule, was very secretive. I guess that made him feel more important. He had contact with a farmer who told him that the two Weicher brothers were alive and hiding at Forester Knopf's house. Moyshe knew Isaac Weicher fairly well. Knopf was the same guy who tried to help us negotiate with the Gestapo to release certain people on August 2, 1942. Isaac had worked for Knopf for several years until Judenfrei, December 1, 1942.

Moyshe told Srul and me about Isaac and his brother Mordche. He said final arrangements were being made for them to join us in a week or so in our new temporary location near our farm. A rendezvous was set up for a definite evening and sure enough Moyshe brought Isaac and Mordche to join us.

Isaac told us that over the years working for Forester Knopf, he had developed a close relationship with Knopf's daughter. It was close enough that when Judenfrei was announced she was willing at her own extreme risk to hide Isaac in her room located on the second floor of the house. The hiding place, according to Isaac, was in the space between the ceiling of the first floor and the floor of her room above. A few days after Judenfrei was declared, Mordche was on his way to report to Turka to be sent to Sambor Ghetto. Isaac wouldn't let him go. He took him back to Knopf's house where both of them stayed hidden.

Isaac told me of the many tense moments they experienced, particularly when the German police would come around to visit Knopf, who was in charge of all the forests in the area. It was Isaac's feeling that old man Knopf was aware that there were two Jews hiding in his house. Finally, it reached a point when it became too dangerous for both parties. Isaac and Mordche had to leave. Isaac knew that Moyshe, Srul and a few others were hiding somewhere in the forest. He also knew about the farmer who had contact with Moyshe. That is how the Weicher brothers came to join our little band of three.

Now we were five and three of us were old veterans at living the way we did. To the newcomers, this type of living was foreign, strange and unpredictable. But they learned fast and found out soon enough what this whole thing was all about—survival.

There were three farmers, Yasio, Juzio and Nikolay, old neighbors of mine, who were very helpful with food and were sympathetic to my problem. They also had a motive. The people in my village were almost totally illiterate. Some had taught themselves to read, word by word, at a snail's pace, a work-worn finger tracing the sentence, stopping on each word. They were religious people, spending a great deal of time reading the bible. They started to talk to me about certain passages in the bible. They told me that there are certain prophecies expressed in the bible. One of the prophecies, the way the farmers interpreted it, was that the Jews will have a great deal of hardship, which will lead to very terrible things, unless they convert, recognize and start believing in Jesus Christ.

Part of the prophecy was becoming a reality thanks to Hitler. I certainly couldn't argue the point. I wasn't even sure they were wrong. What they were saying was literally happening before my very eyes. My neighbors, Yasio, Nikolay and Juzio, implied strongly that I should seriously consider their statements, especially those expressed in the bible. I didn't tell them that the Nazis were also killing converted Jews, as well as individuals with any Jewish blood in them.

When I returned to the forest that night, I told the group about my experience with the farmers. None of us took this episode seriously. A few days later I went back down to the village to get some food. Again, a repetition of the same story, but this time they put a little more pressure on me. They were trying very hard to persuade me to "save" my life. They said the only way to do this is through Jesus Christ. At that point it looked like that was the only logical way.

When I returned, I related the conversion story again to my fellow Jews. The five of us discussed this matter; we played it down, obviously as not a big thing and that I should tell them that this is a serious decision and that I have to think about it.

The next time I saw my neighbors, several days later, I told them that I was seriously considering it and had discussed this matter with Moyshe and Srul. "Give me another week or so and I will have the answer", and then I added, "I am leaning toward doing it". "Why not? After all," I said to myself, "I want to live to see the end of the war." Why am I even hesitating to make a statement to those three guys? Not only will make them happy, but they might come to look upon me as one of them and that may come in handy when I'm in a real bind.

I was brought up in an environment where, between the cheder, my parents and the small Jewish community, it was unheard of to even speak of Jesus. When the topic was brought up, it was met with ridicule. But these were different times. I was no longer a boy. Under the relentless pressure of the times, I had matured with great speed and as a result became much more aware of what life was all about -- especially *my* life. Sure enough a week later, I came down to the neighborhood and as I walked into the farmhouse, I greeted them in Ukrainian, "*Slava Isusu Christu*", which meant "Blessed be Jesus Christ". They were elated. The fact was that I didn't have much of a choice. It was crucial to have them on my side.

Winter was gone and the only snow that remained was high in the mountains in shaded spots where no sun could reach. New grass covered the meadows and farmers had planted crops in the fields. Cattle and horses grazed in the pastures fattening up after a cold winter. Without a calendar I knew that May was ending and June of 1943 was upon us. Had we been hiding out too close to the village too long? How many people knew where we were? Could we continue to trust in all of our neighbors?

The five of us decided to move on to a more inaccessible location and to join the rest of the group, who were now located in the Plishka forest.

Our new location was high up on the steepest part of the Plishka forest wall where the thick brush and bushes gave us more protection. There was no bunker here and we put together makeshift tents. We built our tents under old trees, where, unless the rain was heavy or it was windy, the trees shed some of the rain keeping the area underneath drier than in the open. The tents were put together with the usual triangle type support and were covered with leaves to allow for the rain to run off. Unfortunately, this wasn't as efficient as using tree bark for the same purpose. Bark was the best solution, however, we hardly ever used it, because wherever even a small patch of bark was removed from the tree, it exposed a bright patch of wood that could be seen from great distances. Even with this, it certainly was easier to deal with these types of problems than those we encountered during the winter. The greatest challenge, the only one that mattered, whether summer or winter, the one we faced day in day out—was survival.

Our situation now was more stabilized. This area wasn't readily accessible to outsiders. But we still never knew what could happen. After all, our lives were not really ours; we lived on borrowed time. But life did go on.

And life for David and Elke went on, as well. They were romantically involved. She was a pretty girl and David "grew accustomed to her face". As a man, David needed someone like Elke, but how they handled the intimate moments, I don't know. It must have been much more of a problem during the winter. I never noticed how, where and when, even though we were a closely-knit "family."

While David and Elke were considered a couple by everyone, Aron and Feige started a romance of their own a little later. Someone saw Aron carrying a blanket away from the immediate area and the rumor started to spread. From then on individuals would make fun of Aron and Feige about the blanket. Because of this romantic involvement and the fact that Elke and Feige were sisters, David and Aron were theoretically "brothers in law". I don't think there were any other prospective bachelors who were willing to take on the responsibility of being involved.

David and Aron got along well; David always expressed his opinion in no uncertain terms. Aron, on the other hand, tolerated David's stubbornness because he knew he could never win his case. I'm sure that

Elka and Feige may have had something to do with it. Of course, there was the third sister, Blime. At 16, she was the youngest of the three. Moyshe had his eye on her. She had a nice figure and new how to use it to her advantage. Blime would cater to Moyshe, and for obvious reasons, after all Moyshe was unofficially the leader; everyone looked up to him. It was an honor and privilege to be of service to him. Moyshe, judging from his past, needed a woman; he took advantage of the situation and got closer and closer to Blime. Mind you, Moyshe was more than twice her age. He was old enough to be her father. It was very upsetting that Moyshe had the audacity to take advantage of the situation—pure selfishness—but very few would comment openly.

We all had small makeshift tents and slept in groups of two, three, four or more. Making love became a great deal easier than in the bunker, where such intimate moments were practically impossible. One day shortly after the tents went up Blime became "very" sick and stayed in her tent resting, watched over by her two older sisters, Elke and Feige. Rumor had it that Blime didn't feel well because Moyshe had taken her virginity and, as such a young and inexperienced girl, she didn't handle it very well. After a few days she appeared to recover and emerged from her tent much the wiser. In fact, Blime was now in the driver's seat. Her association with Moyshe gave her a lot of power, which she quickly and unabashedly learned how to manipulate.

Blime made me, as the youngest member of the group, the water carrier or the one to do any other work that had to be done. That was bad enough but she did it in such a disdainful way. It must not have been personal because she treated everyone else in the same manner. For example, we all used the same fire for our cooking. Leibish and Mendel Fuchs would place their pots in the hot coals to cook their meal, which were usually potatoes. When she wanted to cook something, Blime would come along and push their pots aside to put her pots in the best spot. It didn't matter that Leibish and Mendel were more than three times her age. No one dared to contradict her; she was Moyshe's girl.

Even Moyshe took advantage of me. One night in late June 1943, Moyshe and a few others went to Ilnik to get some food -- potatoes and bread, if they were lucky. Because I had been in the village the night before, it wasn't my turn to go. They all returned about 2 or 3 o'clock in the morning. Moyshe woke me up and told me to go down to the edge of the forest, pick up his knapsack and bring it up to our area. That made me angry. More than angry I was frustrated that I couldn't tell him to get lost. I wasn't in a good bargaining position, or so I thought. Frankly, I didn't have to take the abuse from him. He didn't support me; I didn't need any favors from him. I carried my own weight and yet, psychologically, I couldn't tell him off. What hurt even more is that Moyshe was related to me. He was only about 38 and physically much stronger than I was, but that's not what held me back. It was the insecurity within me that made me tolerate Moyshe, which let him take advantage of me.

Warmer days and the beginning of summer gave us more protection in the forest but we still had to go down into the villages far too often to get the food we needed. In early July, a few days after my early morning mountain trudge for Moyshe, several of us went down to the village to get some food and some news, which incidentally we always did. Some went to Ilnik and I went to Radycz. One of the farmers told me that there appeared to be a group, probably Jews, staying in the forest. He also told me about the approximate location. The area was not very far from our camp; just a different part of almost the same forest a few mountains away. I was disturbed by the group's apparent lack of concern for detection. The farmer already seemed to know too much and that wasn't good for them or for us. I needed to find out what else people might know and I asked the farmer to make sure to find out more about that group. We were hungry for information, not only about any other groups that might be near but whether too many strangers knew about them. We couldn't be too careful but we needed to find out what was going on in our area and in the war. At times we got hold of a newspaper and tried to read the stories and read between the lines as well. Often we read with wishful thinking and false hopes.

A few of us came down to the village a few days later and went to the farmer to find out more about this group, whoever they were. We were very concerned because it could affect our own existence. From what we were told, the behavior of the group of Jews left a lot to be desired. What was most disturbing was that the local population all seemed to know all about them as if they were "advertising" their existence. It was obvious to us that they did not know what they were doing; they were literally asking for trouble. *Their* trouble could spell trouble for *us*.

Upon returning to our group, we had a meeting among ourselves to discuss what to do about the situation. We decided to investigate this group, to find them; the question was "how do we find them"—after all, it's a big forest. Having lived in the forest for many months, we had learned how people might function under the circumstances.

Moyshe and I decided to go and investigate. I knew the area well, as well as the people who lived there. We knew approximately where they could be located and went to the forest wall opposite their suspected camp. Moyshe and I settled down to spend the night and wait for the moment when all of us forest dwellers were most exposed to discovery— dawn. We knew that very early in the morning, traces of smoke, even from a well-hidden fire, curled up into the still air. An amateur might miss it but we were not amateurs and neither were those who hunted us. All we had to do was wait patiently until the light was right and then scan the opposite forest wall for those telltale signs. As dawn broke we watched for the slim gray column rising amongst the tall green fir trees. Sure enough, faint traces of smoke drifted up from a steep forest wall across the way.

Our hunch turned out to be right. To get to their location we had to scale down the side of our mountain and cross a ravine in order to climb up the other forest wall where we saw the smoke. Normally, on every occasion the living area of a woodland camp would not be too far from water, whether a spring or a stream, like the one at the bottom of the ravine. I walked in front and Moyshe followed me a few yards behind, as we proceeded up the stream to eventually start climbing the wall of the mountain. As I entered an open area free of bushes, I saw a shabbily dressed man pointing a big gun at me.

"Hände hoch!" Hands up, he shouted.

I raised my hands immediately, facing the rifle. Moyshe followed a few seconds later and immediately recognized the man holding the gun.

"Avrum Feiler", he said as the two embraced and kissed each other.

Gratefully, I lowered my hands and went over to meet Moyshe's friend Avrum. He had been standing guard, protecting his girlfriend Alis, who was washing some clothing in the stream.

Relieved that we were not enemies, Avrum led the way up the mountain toward the rest of the group we had been seeking.

8

The Hunted Become Hunters

We left the clearing by the stream and climbed up the mountain with Avrum Feiler leading the way through the forest. When we reached the encampment, Moyshe and I were surprised to see the size of the group and impressed that they had guns. A gun was a priceless possession (as if that alone could save your life). Avrum introduced everyone and told us that a few of the guys were in the Polish army.

Inevitably, now that we had found each other, the question was "where do we go from here?" Should we merge into one unit or stay separate? We agreed to discuss the matter with our respective groups and meet again in a week or two.

When Moyshe and I rejoined our group and told them about our "find", everyone was pleased. We told them as much about these people as we could especially that most were from Turka and Sambor, not Ilnik and our villages. We discussed merging and in the discussion we recognized some problems. Many in our group had reservations about joining forces with the others. We weighed the arguments for and against combining our.

Those who were against the merger felt that too large a group would make it more difficult to hide. Also, some of us felt that the newcomers didn't have the same philosophy of hiding. *We* were very careful. We didn't think they were as meticulous about details as we were. Not only that, but there was also the possibility that some of them would be too loose with their tongues and could jeopardize our existence.

And more importantly, most of them didn't know this area or any of the farmers.

One argument for merging, however, was that the added number of people could offer more security. Plus, there were several guys who were in the Polish Army who had guns with them. Those could come in handy. The bottom line was—we decided to merge.

The members of their group brought their few possessions and joined us. They began to adjust to very different circumstances not the least of these was our much larger size, more than double what it had been. We shared our makeshift tents with our new companions and built new shelters together on the steep slope of the forested mountain wall. We placed them under the tall trees for added shelter from rain.

The process of getting to know each other and organizing ourselves into this much larger group would take some time, but Moyshe was a leader and some of them already knew him. In spite of our individual and independent way of life, together we needed some sort of loosely organized advisory council to make decisions. Moyshe, with his knowledge of the area and contacts with local farmers, was someone acceptable to the group. Also, he knew one of their trusted men, Avrum Feiler. From our group, the advisory committee added David Berg, who brought his old World War I rifle. With his addition to the council, we now had three Davids on the decision making body of the combined group.

David Binder was street smart, a shrewd operator who thought things over well before he acted. He carried a small revolver with him at all times, not hesitating to kill without regret or guilt. We heard there were rumors circulating that such an event took place shortly before he was transported to the Sambor Ghetto and that the person killed was a Jew from the area. Those who knew what had happened would not talk for whatever reason. I could never get to the bottom of it.

Then there was David Laufer. He was in the Polish army, had a gun, and was bright and good-looking. He walked with confidence, was aware of his good looks and made sure that everyone noticed it. Another armed member of the advisory council was Avrum Liebhart whose nickname was Tatko. I never learned how he acquired that name but that was all anyone called him. He owned an impressive side arm with several bullets. Tatko had a limited education but was street smart.

He did everything at top speed. He ate fast and spoke fast and almost always ended a statement with a question mark, then waited for your reaction with an inquisitive look. From the very beginning Liebhart would look admiringly at Elke and I'm sure he would have been very glad to win her over from Dave Berg, but I don't think Elke was at all interested. Some of the people began kidding him about it.

Then there was Moynie Breitbart, a young guy of about 20. He too had a gun (side arm) which gave him a little extra power. He would do everything fast: walk fast, eat fast and talk fast. He had very definite opinions. It was hard to change his mind, that's why he would run into arguments with others; he meant well but in the process, would make a fool of himself.

Our new forest companions were either from Turka or Sambor but all had one thing in common, they had been sent to the Sambor Ghetto. When all the Jews from Ilnik were rounded up on November 17, the Germans shipped them to the ghetto in Sambor as well, except the few who escaped.

We had heard stories from the farmers but until we met this group from the Sambor Ghetto we had not talked to anyone who had been through the horrors. The two Rosenberg girls were lucky and left in the earliest days. When Isaac and Mordche Weicher joined us, Isaac told us that he had intercepted his brother Mordche on his way to report to the Germans in Turka. You might ask, "at this point, why would anyone willingly report to the Germans?" The answer is that some people simply gave up. It was winter and they lost their will, not only to fight back, but to live. Isaac had a place at the forester's to hide and persuaded his brother to come with him thus saving him from certain transport to Sambor.

As we settled into our new surroundings, we began to hear stories of the gruesome experiences from those who had escaped from the Sambor Ghetto.

◆　　◆　　◆

The Germans used the ghetto as a collection point for all the remaining Jews in the region. The Jews who lingered on after the infamous aktion of August 2, 1942, were Jews who had work permits, *arbeit* permits with the letter A on the armband like the one my mother had arranged for me. Or they were Jews who simply disobeyed the German directive of resettlement. The November 17, 1942 aktion coordinated by the Gestapo, the Ukrainian Police and with the assistance of Jewish police, practically cleansed the entire region of Jews. It was that round up that caught me, but I and a few others from the area, escaped. The unlucky ones who didn't escape were transported by train in freight cars to the Sambor Ghetto.

The Nazis viewed the ghetto as a transitional measure, a storage area holding Jews until they were transported to a death camp or disposed of in less regimented ways. The Germans issued an order that any Jews remaining in the area were to report to the authorities in Turka. From there they would ship them to the ghetto in compliance with the directive that the entire area was to be, as of December 1, 1942, Judenfrei—free of living Jews.

The Jews still resisting the resettlement orders had nowhere to go and no way to get food and shelter as cold and snowy December weather descended on the area. Hungry and cold, they just gave up the fight and reported to the authorities in Turka to be shipped to the ghetto. If not for his brother Isaac's intervention, Mordche Weicher would have been one of those.

Sambor was a large town with an old Jewish district dating from the 15th century. Over 8,000 Jews lived in the old quarter, while the Jews in the Sambor ghetto totaled over 6,000. In the Jewish district now separated from the rest of the town, the Germans crammed all those that arrived from the Turka region into the local jail in extremely overcrowded quarters. Upon their arrival from Turka, about 2,000 of the elderly, men and women, as well as children, were put immediately into cattle cars and transported by train to the Belzec death camp and gassed.

About a month later, in the middle of January 1943, the Germans along with the Ukrainian Police and with the assistance of the Jewish Police rounded up over 1,500 Jews inside the ghetto. Those Jews were then put in the overcrowded jail and from there taken, in groups of 100, to Radlowicz, a swampy area about two miles from the Sambor Ghetto. There the Germans shot them and dumped them into hastily dug pits. Some were not dead. There was a woman and a young boy who survived by crawling out of the pit. The earth was still breathing after a day or two.

During the interludes between roundups, the Jews just waited for the inevitable. While they waited in the overcrowded quarters, some played cards to get their minds off the horror and some told jokes or stories for the same reason. In the streets lay the dead and dying, some from starvation or typhus and others simply tired, too exhausted to resist. The living milled around, hardly paying any attention to the dead in the street.

The wait in the Sambor Ghetto didn't last. Another round-up took place in the early March 1943. Over 1,500 Jews were put in jail and from there in groups of 100 they were taken to the Jewish cemetery and killed by two inebriated Germans. In front of prepared mass graves, with their handguns the two Germans shot the Jews one by one. After each shot the victim fell into the grave.

Some of the Jews in the ghetto saw what was happening and decided to try and escape. They began digging a tunnel, which led into a sewer and outside the ghetto. When they found out that the Sambor ghetto was to be liquidated in a few days they escaped into the countryside and found their way into the mountains where we met them.

The total liquidation of the remaining Jews took place at the end of April 1943. First the Germans and the Ukrainian Police rounded up the regular Jews, searching from house to house and put them in jail. Then they ordered the Jewish Police and the *Judenrat* to report to a certain point in the ghetto. Then the Germans and Ukrainians immediately surrounded the group and put them into the old jail. Then, in groups of 100, they took them to the Radlowicz swamps and killed them all, thus completing the liquidation of the Sambor ghetto.

As I listened to the stories I wondered how different we were. These people from the Sambor Ghetto had wanted to live. They weren't willing to give up their lives without a fight and yet many of them were not what you would call fighters. Amongst our new companions were the tough ones but there were also the timid ones, Hillel Erdman, a middle-aged 45 year-old man afraid of his own shadow; the Schusters, a decent couple, friendly and full of life and Shoil Kleist whose main interest was keeping his belly full. What was it that crushed the will to survive in some but forged a will of steel in others? I knew that my experiences and the tales of these horrors had numbed my humanity but hardened my will to survive.

Our two very different groups now combined to survive the many who hunted Jews, the rigors of living in the wild and the winter. The ghetto survivors had never lived under the conditions that faced them. Because they were unfamiliar with forest living and knew little of the area, they needed our guidance, particularly since we knew the area so well. Many were city people. Most of them had probably never been in a forest, let alone lived there.

The merger created different kinds of problems than we had before. Even though our group included the three Rosenberg girls and Mendel Feiler's wife, their group included nine women. There were several couples who weren't married. They had paired off just as Moyshe and Blime, David and Elke, and Aron and Feige had. Avrum Feiler, Moyshe's friend who greeted us with his gun, had his girlfriend Alis. Itzik Imer was paired with his girlfriend Sally. In the group, there were four married couples: Wolf Donner and his wife, Itzik and Malkah Entner, Favel Stroback and his wife, as well as Schuster and his wife.

Life went on much as it had in the Rostoka forest. At night, we would go to get food either in groups or separately. Those who were not too familiar with the area would invariably be attached to someone who knew his way around. There was one fellow who seldom went with us. Benzion Bernanke was good-looking, knew it and was always showing off. The rest of the group did not pay much attention to him. Impressed with himself, he was always grooming and preening with a comb he carried in his pocket along with a mirror. Although he thought a lot of himself, others did not, considering him lacking in courage. He went out of his way to avoid activities like going to the village to get food or to steal potatoes from farmland. In contrast, Eli Fern, a heavy set, red-faced guy in his late 20's, was not too bright but muscular, which came in handy carrying food to the forest.

At one time I shared a tent with Eli. The tent could accommodate 3, or 4 people. Because our tents were built on steep slopes we had to find ways to stabilize them and at the foot of this one we placed a log that served as support, so as not to slide down the mountainside. We also shared the space with his girlfriend Yadzia, a plain, heavy-set girl about 20 years old. Her older sister Bronia was good-looking, bright and thought a lot of herself. Apparently, David Laufer thought so too and they became a couple.

Sharing one of the makeshift tents with a pair of lovers created a problem. Often, I would be sleeping and the log would rock about while Eli and Yadzia used it for support as they had sex. Not only was it disturbing my sleep but it also stirred my young male instincts to a point where I became very frustrated. Individuals would occasionally change groups for different reasons (not all of them sexual frustration) and I decided to join another group.

Without any regrets I found a place with my Uncle Srul and Schulim Erdman, a person who couldn't kill a fly -- good natured, with the patience of a saint. He was very meticulous, cleaning the outside of the tent as if it was his house in the olden days.

In the daytime we played cards, told jokes, and sometimes listened to Avrom Feiler sing. He sang well, mostly in Yiddish, and everyone enjoyed his entertainment. Some of our new group reminisced about the old times. Others talked about food, good food we had when we were still home. They would describe in detail various tasty foods of all kinds. That was hard to take especially when we were hungry, which was most of the time. The descriptions brought back such memories that our mouths would water. To many of us it was painful.

Having spent almost a year in the forest, I viewed the situation as a normal life in an abnormal world. At times, I would just dream of the things to happen, inviting thoughts as to what it would be like to walk down the street without fear. Suddenly, reality would shatter those thoughts. Of course, no one knew what the next day would bring, let alone the next hour or even the next second. I tried to avoid thinking about my immediate family. It was extremely painful, but sometimes I couldn't help it and my thoughts would take me to my mother. My dear, sweet mother. As the memories deepened, August 2 returned and I saw my mother on the train in the stifling cattle car, with no water, no facilities, nothing. I would have a good cry, which was helpful, washing away the vivid pictures. Then, slowly I would divert my thoughts or take up some physical activity.

As we got to know the people from the Sambor ghetto, they told us of the horrors they had survived. Some talked freely, while others barely spoke of it at all. Unlike our group, many of these people had not known each other before. Avrum Feiler had met his girlfriend Alis in the ghetto. He was the son of a butcher and his family, which was involved in horse trading, never had a good reputation, according to Moyshe who had known him before. However, Avrum was a friendly person with hardly any education, but not a fool. He was also one of the decision-makers in his group. Unfortunately, he wasn't very strong in his convictions and could be easily swayed with a convincing argument. Alis, on the other hand was fairly well-educated and bright with a warm disposition. If it wasn't for the war, I don't think they would have gotten together.

His cousin, Yoshe Schleicher was a Jewish policeman in Turka as well as in the Sambor Ghetto. As a policeman he had taken his job seriously and according to whispers, there were times when he went beyond the call of duty. Some of the stories were pretty ugly. None of those Jews survived.

Yoshe suddenly became very religious. He carried on in a very loud voice with anybody on any subject, in a very dogmatic manner. He always had an opinion and gave you the impression that he was talking down to everyone except for Avrum Feiler and a few others who catered to him. He liked the "*koved*", the honor. He wouldn't eat a chicken if it hadn't been killed in a kosher way by a *shochet* (the man designated to slaughter animals in a humane way). Such hypocrisy. Well, there was no *shochet* in our immediate environment or any environment on this side of the ocean. On several occasions one of his friends would bring him a live chicken. Since there was no *shochet*, he appointed himself as "Rabbi" Schleicher, which would enable him to perform the ritual. It was a sight to behold. There was no razor that looked like a *shochet's* knife. Hillel Erdman had one of those old fashioned razors. When Schleicher found the razor, he literally snapped it out of timid Erdman's hands.

I watched Yoshe Schleicher perform the ritual; it looked exactly the way a real *shochet* would do it, including the prayer required before applying the makeshift *chalef*, the knife or in this case the razor, to kill the chicken. After all Yoshe himself was a butcher before the war and had probably seen on many occasions how the ceremony was performed.

I don't think anyone trusted Yoshe. He was a phony from the word go and would probably sell his own mother to save his life.

Many of the farmers in the area knew what was going on. Some of them were friendly and helpful and would even tell us what they knew. Every once in a while we got a newspaper. As biased as it was, we read between the lines to determine what was happening. We read every word very carefully and if necessary put our own interpretation on an event. We always interpreted what we read in the paper the way we wanted it to be; we were so hungry for good news – even making it up kept us alive emotionally and spiritually.

It's difficult to explain why some of the Ukrainians were willing to risk their lives to help Jews, especially when they were brought up in an anti-Semitic environment. Ukrainians from earliest childhood were indoctrinated with propaganda that Jews were Christ killers and God killers. Because they dressed differently, spoke differently, and prayed differently, they were to be distrusted and hated. And Hitler's spewing all his Nazi hateful propaganda toward the Jews certainly didn't help the situation.

Despite all that, there were a few Ukrainians who took great risks and helped the Jews. Some sympathized with the Jews and some, who actually were anti-Semitic, couldn't sanction murder or genocide. There were Ukrainians who were neutral; they wouldn't help, but they wouldn't hurt. The most feared were those who hated Jews passionately. Many of them participated in massacres of Jews while others drew great satisfaction watching the Gestapo and the police kill Jews.

One farmer in an adjacent village decided to catch Jews, as if we were animals. Besides the obvious reason of hate, there was greed. The Germans and made it worthwhile to catch Jews. The Ukrainian farmers led a very simplistic life, just like their forefathers for generations before them. Tobacco and alcohol were two commodities that most farmers were addicted to from an early age; the Germans knew that.

This particular farmer lived in the middle of Losinits, a suburb of Turka. In mid-July 1943, this farmer caught four Jews including a father and son and kept them overnight. In the morning he planned to deliver then to the police in Turka. The son escaped and notified us. Immediately, Moynie Breitbard and Itzik Eimer went down to the farmer, liberated the three remaining Jews and warned the farmer to stop catching Jews. They told him that the next time he did it he would be killed. He promised in no uncertain terms that he wouldn't do it again.

The farmer evidently didn't take the threat seriously and kept looking for us. He probably thought that catching Jews would make him rich. Perhaps he thought the threat was empty, but that was a mistake -- a fatal one.

Our "high command" decided that the farmer had to be eliminated. We found out from our contacts that the farmer was afraid of retribution and no longer slept at home. That created more of a problem for us because we would have to come into the village in daylight where more villagers might see us. We knew that, from wherever he spent the night, each morning he would have to come and take care of his farm and family.

Summer was passing and there was a smell of fall in the air. As usual, at this time of the year early mornings were foggy. On the chosen morning, Itzik Eimer went down to the farmer's house under the cover of fog. It was unfortunate that the farmer hadn't taken the warning Itzik had given him on the first visit. Perhaps if he had known that Itzik Eimer had been a *kapo* in the Sambor Ghetto he would have paid more attention. *Kapos* were like enforcers, keeping the other Jews in line, supervising the daily activities in the labor camp and the ghetto in Sambor. Itzik gave his fellow Jews a rough time. None of those people whom he roughed up made it. Itzik, like many others, believed that being a *kapo* would save his life and perhaps he enjoyed the power— being somebody. I believe it was a little of both.

A *kapo* was the perfect man for this job. To protect other Jews and ourselves, this farmer had to be eliminated. No more warning. No discussion. There was no point asking whether he had told anyone about us or about our previous visit to free his captives. We knew we had scared him. Apparently not enough to keep him from trying to profit from our condition. Now it was Itzik's job to make good on his threat. The farmer had just come home when Itzik Eimer approached him and killed him on the spot.

Soon after killing the farmer, Moyshe was in the village. As usual, when any of us went into the village, besides getting food, we would always gather intelligence trying to find out what was happening in the world. Even more important was finding out as much as we could about what was happening in the immediate area that could possibly affect us. Moyshe learned from one of the sources that there were farmers from some distant villages asking whether there were any Jews in the area and that they had heard rumors to that effect.

There were two guys from distant villages who traveled quite a long way to look for us. We were afraid that the rumor of "many Jews hiding in the forest" was spreading. We started to see that our biggest fear of the large group making it unsafe was being realized. They hated Jews so passionately that they would travel any distance to catch them for the Gestapo or even kill them like other Ukrainians had. The main reason farmers would travel these great distances was that the Germans gave them rewards. Either way, it was very serious and something had to be done about it without delay.

Through our connections we found out who the men were and where they lived. It was also helpful that one of the guys, Mendel Feller, came from a village close to the location and was familiar with the area. He even knew the two farmers who were trying to make a killing catching Jews.

We wasted no time and picked a night for our mission. Our group included David Binder, Mendel Feller, Srul Felder, Itzik Entner, and others. Because there were three Itziks in the group we sometimes referred to Itzik Entner as the fiyaker. He had owned a horse in prewar Turka and ran a taxi, known in Polish as fiyaker. Itzik was a plain rough guy, very loud with rough language and hardly any education. As one of the armed members of the group, he had a sawed-off rifle with very few bullets, but it gave him the feeling of power. He was just the man for the job.

The village was too far to make it there in one night and return but we walked all night to get close enough to lie up and wait. We stayed all day in a small forest nearby and in the evening, as soon as it became dark we moved into the village and approached his house. Mendel told us that the man we wanted was the son of the farmer. We caught him at home and took him outside. While four men from our group tried to hold him down, he squirmed around trying to escape and somehow slipped out of the jacket and ran. David Binder fired his gun at the escapee and wounded him. Unfortunately, he escaped and we couldn't waste time looking for him.

This frustrated all of us. We had to make sure that these Jew seekers paid a high enough price to discourage them no matter what rewards were offered. If the Germans killed Ukrainians for helping Jews, then we must kill Ukrainians who sought us out for rewards.

In our extreme frustration we took the only action we could and told his parents to get out of the house. We let their two cows and a horse out of the stable, found some gasoline to pour around the buildings, and then lit the fire. Everything went up in flames.

Mendel told us that the other farmer lived several houses up the hill. We were almost certain that the burning farm buildings would warn him and he'd try to disappear. Srul Felder and I decided to run up the hill to see if we could catch him at home. As luck would have it, we saw him through the window and, apparently, he had not seen the flames. We ran back and told the rest that the second guy was home. Quickly, we made it back up the hill and knocked on the door. Just as he opened the door, we grabbed him. Itzik the fiyaker, with his short rifle, shot him right there in the doorway.

Unfortunately, his wife and children witnessed the execution. As terrible as it was, it had to be done. It's the price one pays for survival. It was either him or us—better him. We couldn't take any chances in light of what happened earlier at the first farm. We left the area immediately, walking all night to get back home.

We returned with some sadness, some frustration, some fear and some satisfaction. We all believed that in our small way we were fighting back. More importantly, we believed that our action served notice to others who might seek out other Jews. Psychologically, it turned out well for us. The word spread that the Jews are heavily armed, even though the opposite was the true. That rumor, I believe, definitely enhanced our ability to survive.

9

The Bullets Were Real

There was more to surviving than escaping the Gestapo, the police or vindictive Ukrainian farmers. One of our most formidable enemies was the weather. Our second winter was approaching. In the Carpathian Mountains, winter can start as October and last until late April or early May. It was like being in a prison; we had no freedom of movement. The first winter, we were not properly clothed. Our shoes were torn and our clothes in such a dilapidated condition that they offered little protection from dry penetrating cold and the freezing wind. There wasn't a moment when I didn't believe that without better clothes we wouldn't survive the coming ordeal. But, how would we get warmer jackets, heavier slacks and shoes without holes.

Without the group that joined us from the Sambor Ghetto and the few guns they had, we would never have entertained the thought of robbing someone just for warm clothing for the winter. It was a matter of survival. Considering all our options, the elders made the decision to do just that. The target was a wealthy farmer in the village of Dolzki. Isaac and Mordche Weicher once lived in that area so they knew the farmer fairly well and told us there was a chance he might have a gun.

Dolzki was somewhat removed from the area where we stayed. That was one of the reasons we picked it. The fact that the Weichers knew the area and the wealthy farmer sealed the choice. We could not expect to find winter clothes in any abundance in a poor farmer's home and with the risks we were taking we needed to be assured of success.

We had to make our raid in one night. About 15 of us left camp early in the evening to reach Dolzki before midnight. We arrived there at about 11pm and approached the farmhouse. At the front of our rag tag group, Avrom Feiler, in a German style coat, looked menacing with his big gun in his hands. Fat Eli looked impressive in a Russian Army raincoat while the rest of us were dressed in our usual torn clothing.

Avrum Feiler banged on the farmer's door and announced that we were the police and to open up. The farmer on the inside asked who it is.

"Aufmachen. Policei", repeated Feiler in a clear loud voice ordering the man to open the door.

When he opened the door we forced the farmer back inside. Then we ordered him and his family to lie face down on their bed and not to move or make any noise if they cherished their lives. Every one of us looked for warm clothing. Avrum Feiler and David Laufer pressed the owner for guns that we had heard he had. Unfortunately the farmer wouldn't admit that he owned any guns and there wasn't much we could do about it. We set about finding things we needed or wanted and took all sorts of clothing, men's woolen jackets and trousers as well as nice women's garments, blouses, and skirts. I found a warm winter jacket. God only knew how I needed it.

Feiler directed the operation; he decided what we should take. We gathered food, breads and cheeses but what really stood out was honey. The farmer had his own beehive and his industrious bees had presented him with a huge pail of honey. We took the whole pail even though it was too heavy for one man. When everyone was ready, we loaded up with all sorts of goods, clothing and food, and we left the farmhouse. Avrum Feiler told the farmer and his family not to get up until daylight and then we disappeared. As far as they were concerned, we came from nowhere and left to nowhere.

Our raid was successful except we got no guns. We headed for our Plishka Forest camp carrying all manner of loot, especially the huge pail of honey. It took two of us to carry our golden treasure and we constantly kept on switching partly to relieve the burden and partly to sample the sweet nectar. Whoever carried the pail had his finger in the honey—licking. By the time we reached home base, half of the honey in the pail was gone and everyone had sticky remnants on their hands and faces. It was irresistible.

When we came back from the robbery, everyone had a story to tell; what each one did in the participation of the robbery, especially the carrying of the honey and the licking. It was a light-hearted moment. Those of us who went on the raid supplemented our meager clothes with the newly acquired pieces even sharing with those who didn't have enough. Although we mainly looked out for ourselves, we still felt some sympathy for others in our group. It was impossible to say how far that would go when our individual survival depended upon a single-mindedness to stay alive at all costs.

It's amazing what normal human beings will do when put in a situation like this. The Nazis looking for us had no remorse, not one ounce when it came to taking our lives. But these "crimes" we had to commit to seemingly innocent Ukrainians, filled us with remorse, but it was not long-lasting. Our lives were on the line every second of everyday. We hated to steal and we felt bad for the farmer, but we had no choice. He had plenty and we had nothing. We also worried about the possible consequences that might develop. There were all sorts of theories advanced about what might happen if the farmer decided to look for us, or if some one had seen us. Maybe they would try and find us. But that was the way we lived now. People were trying to find us and kill us. That was the fact. The bottom line was that we had to do it and had to live with it.

As far as the original group was concerned, we had been hiding now for almost a year and this life was taking on a kind of normal existence. We knew the precarious position we were in, but somehow we refused to acknowledge it. More and more we believed that there was a strong possibility that we might make it. When we got a newspaper, which was not too often, the news was certainly much better. Reading between the lines, we could clearly see that things were not going too well for the Germans. There was more hope that one day soon we would be able to walk down the street in daytime without fear. We were also mindful that we were not supposed to be here or anywhere for that matter. A horrible and frightening thought indeed.

On our trips to the villages, we often picked up valuable information from friendly farmers who told us of rumors and stories, many of which filled in details that we would have never found out in our isolation. David Binder learned that the fellow he shot at had not escaped unharmed but had been wounded in the testicles and wound up in the hospital. The rest of the information was less exact. Some said that he escaped unharmed. We actually never found out.

Every once in a while, Mordche Weicher would cheer us up by performing a broadcast of the latest news from Moscow radio in Russian. It was a delight to listen to it, because that was exactly what we wanted to hear. He would transmit the news from the front and relate how the heroic Red Army was inflicting heavy casualties on the Germans. He would even give us the location where the battle took place and relate how the soldiers of the "super race" were being beaten by ordinary soldiers of the Soviet Union.

It was strange how simple things took on great meaning. In the past, I wouldn't have given it much thought, but here in the mountains, without any basic comforts, even the drinking water took on an exaggerated importance. I'll give you an example. Mordche Weicher (the one who couldn't kill a fly) was well educated, most likely better than anyone in the group and a man with the patience of a saint. Water was always scarce and had to be carried up the mountain from the river. We could get water from little springs close by where we stayed but they bubbled up from the ground at a snails pace. Few of us had the patience to collect that water drop by drop. I had watched Mordche next to one of those springs with a spoon trying to capture the drops of water and pour them into a cup. Needless to say, it took a great deal of time and patience to fill a small cup with water.

Hours of inactivity and boredom with frequent scares of discovery needed the kind of relief that humor provides. Humor at the expense of someone annoying was all the more delicious. Itzik Entner was a loud mouth, so some of the guys looking for a little entertainment would kid around with him. On one occasion they made him a proposition. If he shaved off his pubic hair with the guys as witness to the event, they would give him three kilos of flour. With such a small price to pay for so much flour, he willingly applied his razor. Itzik Entner was one of the few who had his wife with him. As his prickly stubble of new hair began to grow back, those guys and others would kid him about the fact that he could not have relations with his wife until the pubic hair grew in soft. On another occasion, since Itzik could not stop talking, the guys made another deal with him. They told him if he stopped talking for one hour they would give him flour. Guess what? Itzik lost.

One of the big preoccupations in the forest day and night, summer and winter was the search for lice. We would always be on a search and destroy mission. Lice were every where, in the hair, under the arms, in private areas but the most favorite spot was in our clothing, our *shmates,* the rags that we wore. There they rested, multiplied, and attacked our bodies sucking our blood. Rabbits have nothing on lice in multiplication. They multiply with frightening speed in a geometric progression. I believed, if not controlled, they would inherit the world. There was no soap or ample water or a place to wash, particularly in the wintertime. The lice hid in the seams laying eggs, and multiplying. As fast as they grow, they look pretty full at about an eighth of an inch, particularly when they get satisfied with your blood. When it gets pretty bad and itchy, I would squeeze them with my nails but I would never succeed killing all of them in one spot.

In the summertime, the killing of lice was somewhat more efficient. It was easier to wash our clothes, which eliminated some of the lice. When possible, drying our clothes in the hot sun really reduced their numbers. But the best method was to hold the garment over a fire or preferably over coals hot enough to make the lice move to get out of the heat. As they crawled, the lice couldn't hold onto the garment and would fall into the fire or hot coals. As we shook the garment, the lice fell onto the coals and burst creating a popping sound. With so many of them falling into the flames, the sound was similar to a machine gun firing.

There was monotony to our life in the forest. We spent the day quietly doing the few things that we needed to exist. The senses rested almost like forest animals with one eye open and ears cocked, ever alert for the danger unseen but ever present. We were never completely relaxed even during moments of laughter and storytelling. We existed. Sometimes we would spend days without anything unusual and then in a blink of an eye we would be shocked into that momentary focus of fear. Run. Hide. False alarm. It had a strange effect, a kind of exhaustion that drained the spirit. I was sort of numb, my body was frozen emotionally; all I knew was that I wanted to live; I wanted to see the end of the war. As bad as things were, being drained physically and mentally, somehow deep inside me I was sure I was going to make it. I could not explain it but I knew it was true.

The days were getting shorter; the nights were getting cooler, sometimes quite cold. It was time to think of a bunker; tents would not see us through a hard winter. Whatever little freedom of movement we had was going to be curtailed to a large extent. We had to think about what was coming. It was a horrible thought—the approaching winter. I remembered the first winter and knew that this one would be worse. Our survival—my survival gave me concern. It would be harder. Each day was harder and more dangerous if for no other reason than the threat of discovery.

Our life was one of constant insecurity. It didn't take much to put a good scare into us at point. We were tired and edgy and not looking forward to our struggle with the winter snows. One night, in preparation for days of impassable drifts, a few of us were going to the village to collect and bring back food to store for winter. As we were going through the bushes, the trigger on David Berg's ancient gun caught a twig and the gun went off. We were all frightened to death, but soon we realized that this was David Berg's gun. The gun was very old, of WWI vintage and not well taken care of. The barrel was rusty, especially the chamber. When the gun discharged, the shell stuck in the chamber so badly that David couldn't pull it out. He finally had to get it out using a rod—a "miracle".

Some of our leaders, Moyshe, Feiler and Binder went to explore and look for a proper location for a bunker in the Rostoka forest. That was the same general area where we started off the first winter. As usual, the place had to be in an area not too far from water, not easily accessible, and a place where a farmer would have no reason to go. From our side of the forest wall, we would have to be able to see anyone approaching from the opposite mountain wall of the forest. This time we were thinking of how to arrange it so that we would not have to go to the village and worry about the tracks in the snow and everything connected with it.

We found what we thought would be a desirable spot and started to build a bunker in Rostoka. This was our second winter in the forest and, with our previous experience, we took our time and tried to anticipate any problems we might encounter. Everyone was being very helpful.

One of the things we thought we should have was a hand-mill. Then we could grind grain into flour to bake bread cakes. A friendly farmer gave us one. Such a hand-mill is very heavy and it took a great deal of manpower and effort to get the sucker to the bunker. In a relatively short time we accumulated plenty of grain, potatoes and related items. The fewer times we had to go into the village minimized our chance of discovery. By the middle of November and early December 1943 we thought that we had completed everything to the best of our ability. Everyone was very hopeful.

In the beginning of January 1944, Moyshe or David had to go down to the village. One of our Ukrainian friends told him that there were rumors that the Germans know our location and it is only a matter of time before they come and try to catch us. Generally, our informants seemed to have had reliable information. We could not ignore the warning.

This was devastating news and a serious concern for everyone. Even if it was only a rumor we could not afford to take chances. Deep snow covered the mountain wall, drifting higher along the valleys and ridges. After preparing to go into the snows as little as possible, a move now would be extremely difficult. Besides, where do we go, how do we get there and how do we do it? We have no food for any prolonged period of time; we don't have proper clothing or shoes. Whether we have the energy to walk across these mountains was a question only the trek would answer. One point was clear. We had to get out of where we were.

Moyshe, the Weicher brothers and a few others familiar with other parts of the forests decided to move east approximately 10 to 15 miles to a place in the Zadowbane Forest.

The winter sun disappeared behind the mountain bringing an early darkness to the Rostoka Forest. Since it was safest to travel at night, for once winter offered us extra hours. We would need them for our long trip. Everyone took as much as they could carry. We left as it started to get dark and walked all night through the snow until we reached our destination. It was a flat piece of the Zadowbane Forest. There was no time to start searching for a "good spot" according to our specifications. We were all exhausted; there wasn't even a place to lie down.

Everything was white, even the trees surrounding us were covered with their mantle of snow. The ground, the rocks, the scraggly bushes were gleaming with snow. I stood like an idiot among the trees, one of the few things that weren't camouflaged by winter's snow. You hear a noise and you wonder if it is a bird or someone who has already spotted us. Like the wild forest animals, you become alert to the smallest sound and listen with attention to a point of paranoia. Finally you are convinced; it was no one, only a bird flying by.

Immediately after clearing snow from a spot of ground, we started to set up a makeshift tent to accommodate the group. It took about two days to complete our new quarters. At the same time we were running out of food. We had been unable to carry more food because we had to carry all the basic equipment to build our shelter. All the while, new snow fell over the forest and mountains making it impossible to go back to the old bunker for supplies or to the village to fetch some food. We were in a very precarious situation.

While all this was happening, we said prayers in the morning as well as in the evening. Most people participated in the prayer, even those who weren't religious. I suppose they must have found some inner satisfaction in it. Some of us, including me, questioned this whole prayer business. Logically it didn't make any sense. Praise God, exalt him, thank him; for what? Look at the position we were in. If there is a God, how does he allow this to happen? And if there is no God, why pray? Someone said praying may not help but it certainly can't hurt. Either way it is a confusing philosophy. But praying went on day in and day out. Ironic, huh?

Yoshe Schleicher appointed himself as the Rabbi of the "temple in the snow" and made sure that we said prayers. Prayer or no prayer, we had a job to do -- how do we get food?

Yoshe Schleicher always carried around his sawed-off gun, for which he only had several bullets. God forbid he had to use it. He didn't move without it, as if this would save his life against all odds. I wasn't minimizing the value of possessing a gun. Owning a gun was extremely important. I wished I'd had one. Yoshe carried this gun around with such a disdainful attitude, as if saying, "You folks here are perhaps safer than anyone else because of my presence". He probably believed it—that it was the praying and his gun. Yoshe never did any physical work; he was there, you might say, in a "supervisory" capacity. Yoshe was a close relative of Avrum Feiler and therefore could afford to carry on with those types of stupidities. No one would dare to talk back to him. Unfortunately, Yoshe had no solution to our problems.

What we needed was some sort of a Moses to get us out of there—but that was wishful thinking. "What do we do now", was the question? The only way to make the food operation feasible was to ski. Skis were the answer. There was no other way to get out of the area. How could we make skis?

Avrum Feiler, David Binder, Mendel Feller, and David Laufer put their heads together. We had enough equipment to "fabricate" skis and before two or three days were over we had skis. They weren't professional skis by any means, in fact far from it—better described, they were a joke. Some of the people in the group had never been on skis. What we actually needed was a means to stay on top, or walk on top of the snow, if you will. Somehow the guys built a few pair of skis that allowed our able-bodied companions to ski, walk, or even crawl across the snow well enough to get to the other bunker to bring back food.

We had supplied the bunker at Rostoka with enough basic necessities to minimize the dangerous trips to the village. One of our valued possessions was the hand-mill for grinding grain into flour. To make flour out of the grain was a tedious and difficult undertaking and the hand-mill was too heavy to move to our new place at Zadowbane. We would start skiing late afternoon, arrive at the bunker within 4 to 5 hours, we would rest a bit, and start to produce flour by taking turns at the mill. We would stay there during the day, load ourselves up with supplies, get back on the skis and return to Zadowbane the following night.

The way some of the guys skied, was a sight to behold. When you saw Aron Hans on skis it was hilarious. He had never skied in his entire life and he had two left feet which did not help the situation. There were hills and valleys. Some of us were able to ski downhill, but others just couldn't do it. They would come down sideways or they would just slide down on their fannies. It was really funny and would have been a great joke if it had not been so serious—it was a matter of life and death. We did this for about a month and a half.

Finally, we couldn't produce enough flour, so we were forced to bring whole grain back to our camp. There was no salt and eating whole grain without salt was impossible; I just couldn't eat it and got weaker and weaker. I was in a group with the Weichers. Mordche would try to help me but what could he do. Somehow they were able to eat the stuff but I couldn't, even though I knew that I had to eat to survive.

One day Moyshe ventured out and went to the village, first to find out what was happening in the world and also to get some food. Moyshe brought back some bread and pork. Every one looked out only for himself. There was no sharing. I noticed that and even though I was really weak and Moyshe knew it, neither he nor his girlfriend Blime offered me any.

I noticed that Blime took the pork, went outside the tent, walked away about 50 feet and hid it in the snow. I knew if I could get a hold of some of that pork it could change my life. I kept a close eye on where that pork was hidden without raising any suspicion of what I had in mind. The question was, "how do I do it and when?" I found a used razor blade; I believe it belonged to Isaac Weicher. I figured out that the best opportunity was while most of the people were praying and as it was getting dark. I chose the moment and quietly slipped away to the place where Blime hid the pork. I cut it in half, more or less, and returned to the tent, where I went over to the corner and put it under my jacket.

Soon Mordche cooked the grain, handed it over to me and said that I must eat. I took the cooked grain, moved over into the corner, cut some of the pork into my dish and, boy oh boy, it made a big difference. All of a sudden it tasted delicious. I kept that pork hidden and used it sparingly and surreptitiously for about three to four days. I came back to myself; it was a miracle. Blime discovered the theft but not the thief and nothing happened.

Dave Berg and Moyshe Hans went down a few more times to the village to get food but also to find out about the news. We were keenly aware that the Germans were not doing too well on the eastern front. There was talk about the Allies opening a second front, but nothing was really happening, except for Africa where the Allies scored some significant victories.

There was no question that it was only a matter of time and Germany will be defeated. We didn't have the luxury of time. We were deep in this God-forsaken place. The big question was: "will we live to see the end of the war?" We were so close and yet so far, as the saying goes.

Life in this place on a daily basis was so abnormally "normal", as if this was the way it was supposed to be. We prayed; we ate whatever was available; we joked; we laughed at ourselves; we laughed at each other. We hardly brought up that we were scared or the topic of fear itself, even though it was there continuously; we just tried to ignore it, if such a thing is possible.

We rarely went to the village because of security -- the fear of discovery. In mid-February 1944, we found out from one of farmers in the village, on one of the infrequent visits, that the Germans came using skis to look for us. They told us that the Germans found some traces in the snow; however, they could not get very far in their search because on top of the mountains the wind blows much stronger and erases any activities in the snow. They returned to the village "empty handed". While all of us were very pleased to hear that they couldn't continue their search, we were also concerned. Would the Germans come back? We knew they would but how soon. Suddenly we faced a threat even more pronounced. We had to move again. But in February, in our part of the country, winter is at its most severe and the thought of moving anywhere was impossible.

It was almost the middle of March and there was no sign of new searches by the Germans. Perhaps they had given up looking for us while snow was still on the ground. For whatever reason they had not shown up again. We thought that there was just a chance that they might not show up at all. It was definitely a risk; but so was our existence. We began entertaining the idea of moving back into the original bunker, where we still had supplies and were closer to a friendlier village. A big plus was that we wouldn't have to use skis. We made a decision and a couple of days later we were back in the old Rostoka bunker.

There was still two feet of snow on the ground but it was easier to get down and back to the village than the five-hour ski trip. On March 21, 1944, only a few days after our return to Rostoka, I returned from the village bundled in my warm woolen jacket that I stole from the rich farmer. I was tired. It was early, about four in the morning, and cold when I entered the bunker and stretched out in the clothes I was wearing, too weary to care. My jacket was warm and I fell deep into sleep.

Four hours later, machine gun chatter and the terrible noise of an attack filled the bunker. I woke up momentarily disoriented. Then I realized what was happening. The Germans had arrived and I was alone. Everyone had fled. I was the last guy in the bunker. I shot out of the bunker as fast as the bullets from the German's guns. My old motto was that if I am destined to get a bullet, it should come in the back; I couldn't possibly think of facing it.

As I ran out of the bunker, I started straight up the hill, running past trees and anyone also trying to escape. I ran past everyone. It was everyone for himself. Some of the people were slower, especially the women. No one could do anything for anyone else. The machine guns kept firing away, bullets whistling past us as we ran.

I could hear another gun somewhere below. It was David Laufer. He had a fairly good gun with some ammunition and was firing back at the Germans from behind a tree. His opposing fire drove the Germans back down too low on the opposite side of the mountain wall where they lost accuracy when firing at us. They were not experienced enough in mountain fighting to aim differently and they were firing above our heads. Schuster's pregnant wife could not run fast enough up the hill and she did not make it. Because of his action, David Laufer saved most of our lives. I could hear his gun and the return fire of the German machine guns. Then David's gun was silent.

I was the first one to emerge from the trees reaching the top of the mountain. Others, those possessing some common sense, would zigzag from tree to tree taking shelter in between, particularly those that were in the Polish Army. One of the reasons that I was not as careful as I might have been or should have been was that I had that feeling inside me that the bullets the Germans were firing were not real bullets and that nothing will happen to me. When I reached the treeless top of the mountain, I stopped and hesitated. What to do next? By then most of the others had caught up with me. We had a dilemma: "should we go to the other side of the mountain wall?" That meant crossing the open area. "Or should we wait to see what was happening?" We didn't have too many choices. I was the first one standing in the snow at the edge of the forest. This could be an entrapment by the Germans. I had to think fast.

Somehow I felt fearless, I thought if this was an entrapment then there was no chance of getting out of this mess, but if it was not an entrapment, then we had to get out of this place in a hurry. I was the first one to cross the open area and I couldn't move too fast in two feet of snow even if I wanted to. Every one followed and before we knew it we were in the other side of the forest. This was somewhat of a relief, but we were also very discombobulated.

10

Desperation

We crossed over to the other mountain wall, running when we could, climbing up and then down again, moving away from the Germans and our old bunker. I didn't know where we would find shelter but reaching the safety of a distant part of the forest was my first thought.

We could no longer hear the guns, partly due to distance and partly because we had reached another mountain wall shielding us from our pursuers. We pressed on, moving along the lower slopes of the third mountain. We couldn't run any farther. Exhausted, hungry and confused, we needed to rest. The forest was silent; there was no sound of the Germans.

Most of us ran out of the bunker with the clothing on our backs, just the barest essentials and nothing to eat. I was fortunate because I fell asleep in my warm jacket. I was sharing this jacket with Isaac Weicher on and off. His brother Mordche was almost barefoot. There were others who had little protection on their feet. Some had soleless leather shoes, which when wet were slippery and when freezing were rock hard. My shoes were so full of holes that snow pushed inside cold and wet, soaking my feet as I ran. There were two little girls with us (Avrum Feiler knew their parents who placed the girls with a neighboring farmer. Avrum found the girls and brought them to our group). Only six and eight, the two little girls Chavele and Estie had trouble moving in the deep snow and by the time we reached safety on the far side of the third mountain, their toes were frozen. Everyone had his or her story to tell and none was pretty.

It was freezing. We barely had enough clothes before the attack and now we had even less to fend off the cold. We had nowhere to go. If we knew what was happening we might make decisions but we knew nothing. Had the Germans followed us after the attack? They could easily find our early trail in the snow. Were the Germans still in the village? Were they waiting for us or searching for us? We had no idea; we were full of fear. Here we were in the middle of a forest, in deep snow waiting—waiting for a possible attack. It could happen any minute, perhaps any second; what a hopeless and helpless situation to be in. We walked aimlessly through the woods all day. No one wanted to venture into the village. We just had to stay out of sight.

In the evening I went to a farmer to get some food for the others. This farmer knew me and my parents and I trusted him, but cautiously. I had no choice; I had to do it. The farmer didn't have that much but I managed to bring back some food for our group. A few boiled potatoes and some coarse oat bread were all he could offer but to us it was manna from heaven. We had a little something to eat and then talked. We all agreed that we had to disperse.

There was no way we could begin to put together any sort of a bunker or shelter. We had no food, no equipment, and most importantly no safe place suitable to start a new bunker. Those people who knew farmers who might take them in and hide them said they would do that. Others, who knew no one in the area, didn't have a choice. They would stay in the Plishka Forest in the open air. Among that group were Isaac Weicher and Mordche Weicher, Yidl Feller and Berl Feller, Leibish Abel, Mendel Fuchs and Shaye.

I couldn't imagine how they would survive in the open air without food and no way of getting it. Not knowing any of the farmers in the area, they couldn't go down to a farm or village under cover of darkness and ask for food. Neither could they steal any under the circumstances. I feared for their lives.

What was *I* going to do? I was quite desperate to find a place to hide. I remembered my neighbor Yohana who helped me the year before when I was in a very similar situation. The weather was much colder than last year. Again, I took a chance. I wasn't sure she would agree to let me stay there. Exhausted, undernourished and frightened, I must have appealed to her protective instincts and in spite of the danger she took me in. She agreed to let me hide for a few days in the stable. I hid in the attic where the hay was stored. Perhaps she remembered our sexual encounter from last year. A normal warm meal felt like heaven on earth and did wonders for me sexually and otherwise.

Rumors moved fast in the small villages. I found out that on their way back, the Germans, frustrated at not disposing of the Jews hiding in the forest, went into one of the houses at the outskirts of Ilnik and killed the farmer in front of his seven children. We frequently went to that farmer for food and he was very helpful to us. Whether they knew that or just took revenge on the nearest farmer, I didn't know.

On the fifth day, Yohana told me that the Germans were heading this way. They were coming up the village to make sure that the farmers who had horses used them to deliver lumber for the war effort. Yohana owned a horse. Every time Germans came to the village for any particular purpose, they would always search the house and everything else connected with it. I was in the hay and asked myself, "What do I do? If I stay and take a chance, that could be the last thing I do and in addition I could get the woman who gave me a chance in deep trouble. Yohana might possibly lose her life." I made a quick decision and ran out of the house in the middle of the day, something I had not done in almost a year and a half. Hoping no one saw me, I headed up the still snow covered hill. In spots the snow was already starting to melt, but unfortunately there were few trees to hide behind. That bothered me, but soon I was on top of the mountain. As I rested a little behind one of the few trees that were there, I saw the Germans walking up the village. I was happy being where I was, I almost felt like a bird in the air, instead of in the hay.

"Now, where do I go?" It was still cold even though the sun was getting stronger. Though pleasant in the daytime, the nights were extremely cold. I was alone; I had nothing except what I had on, which wasn't much.

There was no place for me to go. When we split several days before, I overheard Avrum Feiler, David Binder, Tatko and one or two others say that they were going to the "Mama", a nickname for mother, not her real name, but a woman living in the adjacent village of Losinic. Avrum

Feiler and the others knew her from before. She was a poor woman who lived in an isolated house, not too close to the village (which was good) but on a plateau that could be seen from far away and not too close to trees. This was a negative. But I didn't have a choice and took a chance. At dusk, I went there. I don't think the guys were too happy to see me, but they let me stay there overnight. The little girls, Chavele and Estie were no longer with Avrum. He had brought the two girls into the mountains when his friends—their parents—were killed. They were mature for their years but they were a liability to the group as a whole now that we had lost the bunker and were on the run. Both girls had lost parts of their toes from frost bite during our flight from the bunker and Avrum found a safer place for them with a family in Losinic.

The next day, Avrum and the others said that I must leave because it was too risky. They were leaving too, but I couldn't go with them. I suspected they made the statement just to get rid of me. They didn't want to have someone to drag along because ultimately it was everyone for himself, no matter what. It was my feeling that they thought their chances of survival were better and they didn't want anyone else to have this possibility. Crazy, perhaps, but definitely true.

I was desperate. I didn't know where anyone was: not Moyshe, not Uncle Srul or the rest of the "gang". I was completely alone; it was a miserable feeling. As lonely and as miserable as I was, I wasn't about to give up. My drive to go on was stronger than ever.

I thought of a poor woman who lived in Ilnik. Her house was removed from the village, which was good from my point of view -- less traffic, less exposure. However, the house was located in an open area. There was no protection in case I had to run. There were no trees to hide behind and it was not easy to tell if anyone was approaching unless they were on top of you. However, the distance of her house from the village was one of the reasons I thought of her. She used to work for my parents on occasion. Her husband was a thief. He used to beat her up a lot and was probably why she had no teeth.

When I went to her house and asked her for shelter, her husband wasn't there; in fact, he was in jail. That was good because I didn't think I could trust him as much as her. She was afraid to keep me, but she let me stay for the day. I was glad for the temporary shelter and was relieved that she didn't leave the house. That's how I knew she didn't report me. I left in the evening.

Again, I was in the same dilemma. I had to decide where to go and didn't have too many choices. There were a few farmers that would help me out with food, like the ones that tried to convert me, but they were afraid to let me stay. If the Germans found me hiding with a farmer, we would both meet the same deadly fate.

There was one more place to try. I thought it might work out. The farmer, a man named Ivan, lived with his wife and 4 year old daughter. They were a poor family, living halfway up the side of a mountain. The farm was barren land; too poor to produce anything. Ivan worked for rich farmers, at one time including my parents. He would cut lumber for use in homes. This was the only fuel available for cooking and heating. In the fall he would cut wheat, thrash it and do other menial work. His wife had helped my mother with the laundry, which was always a big undertaking, especially in the wintertime. Without electricity, all laundry had to be done by hand and was a time-consuming job. For a day or so, the laundry would soak in big, big pots. Then they would boil it before carrying it down to the river where they scrubbed it and beat it with a bat to get the dirt out. The routine was the same even in the wintertime. After that, it was rinsed and hung on ropes in the back of the house, or in the attic.

It was unlikely that anyone would visit Ivan and his family, which meant more safety for me. Another good reason to try and stay there: The house was strategically located overlooking the village. More like a hut than a farmhouse, it was a palace to me, under the circumstances.

In utter desperation I went to see them. They were glad to see me; they fed me with whatever little they had and then asked me where I was going. A question I expected, but was hoping they would not ask. I spoke to them and told them that I would provide food for all of us and I asked them if I could stay until the weather warmed up a little. It was late March or early April and the days were getting longer. There were indications that the spring was in the air, but the nights were still very cold.

I was so thankful not to be living out in the open, in deep snow; I had found a haven. One night about a week later, a sudden knock on the window scared the hell out of me. I thought I had reached the end of the line. Fortunately, it turned out to be Moyshe and Srul. I was glad to see them, but at the same time I was angry that, with all their contacts, they came to invade my domain, so to speak. They weren't concerned about me when we dispersed. Somewhere along the line I must have mentioned this farmer to Moyshe and this is how they found me. It was likely that they were looking for a place to stay and not for me.

We stayed together for about three weeks until the snow began to melt. When the farmers from the village came to work their lands all around us, it was not safe for us to stay there any longer. In fact, on a few occasions we had to go up to the attic to avoid detection.

While I stayed at Ivan's farm, the snow was originally quite deep, somewhere between 2 and 4 feet. I used to go to the village to fetch food and keep my promise that I would provide the food while I stayed there. My problem was that I had to pass my house, both on the way to get food and on the way back to Ivan's farm. All the villagers used the road in front of my house. Those 200 yards were extremely dangerous because anyone could recognize me and I could fall into the wrong hands. There was no way for me to detour.

I couldn't go too early because of the possible "traffic". Going too late could be too suspicious. My heart almost stopped beating every time I passed my house. This was where I spent my childhood. I knew every tree, every rock, every bend of the stream. This was where I played as a little kid. Now I have to talk by my beloved home as a 16 year old fugitive. I was literally numb; I couldn't allow myself to become too emotional; I was psychologically frozen. But I knew, without a doubt, what I wanted. I wanted to live; I wanted be able to walk down the road again without fear; I wanted live to see the end of the war. I had to try and stay focused on what I was doing.

One night I went to the farmer as usual to get food and on the way back I passed my house. I had another 50 yards to go before turning off the road to go up the hill to Ivan's farm. Suddenly, I heard horses and sleds approaching. It was late. "What was coming?" I was puzzled and suspicious. "Who would be on the road at night?," I thought to myself. There were rumors that Ukrainian Nationalists were roaming the villages. The instinct to survive raised the worst fears in me.

In spite of the German's Judenfrei orders from December 1942, the area was not free of Jews. We were still here and the Germans knew it. Did the Ukrainian Nationalists know where we were or were they chasing rumors? They still hunted Jews—if there were any left, officially or otherwise. They hunted all their enemies, the Communists, the Poles and now the Germans who once had been their friends. At least they thought the Germans were their friends but now knew otherwise. But it was us, the Jews, they hated the most.

I was dressed like a poor farmer, carrying a fairly heavy bag and I spoke Ukrainian like any Ukrainian. As they approached, I stepped aside into the snow to let them pass because the road was wide enough just for the sleds. The two men in the sleds stopped in front of me, looked at me and asked my name. I didn't hesitate and told them my neighbor's name. I must have been acting well. Evidently, I satisfied their inquiry and they just drove off. I couldn't believe it. "This is what makes a good spy," I thought to myself. I was very pleased with having passed inspection, but my legs were trembling, ready to collapse.

I began to realize that there are no heroes. The circumstances make one a hero. At the moment of the event I did what I had to do to become that person you are supposed to be. It is strange, but as I answered the question I was convinced I was that person.

I continued on my way for another 50 yards or so and then turned off the road heading for Ivan's farm.

While Moyshe, Srul, and I stayed at the farm, Uncle Srul became sick. I thought it might be a cold and knew that chicken soup would help. That was always my mother's prescription. There wasn't much to eat, mainly potatoes and sometimes a little bread so I went down to the village determined to steal a chicken. The snow was pretty much gone. I went to a neighbor's farm and sneaked into the stable where the chickens were quietly roosting for the night. I caught a chicken by the throat. What squawking. I had to choke it to stop the noise but the other chickens began squawking. I ran out of the stable and raced up the hill with the dead chicken in my hand.

At the farm, I took out my penknife and cut the chicken's throat. I was pretty sure that my uncle wouldn't eat the chicken if he knew that I choked it—not kosher. For a bit it bothered me almost as much that I cut the throat of a dead chicken as it did for not telling my uncle the truth. At any rate, Uncle Srul had some soup; in fact we all did. Farmer Ivan's wife went down to the village the next day. When she returned, she mentioned what she heard that someone was trying to steal chickens but there was no reaction and the subject never came up again. A couple of days later Uncle Srul felt better.

We left Ivan's farm because there were so many farmers working the field all around us. We wanted to hook up with the Russian partisans. There were rumors circulating that they were near but we could not find them.

We came back to the old Plishka forest area and rejoined the group that had been living there under the skies in the open since the attack. They told us that they had a fire going in the snow and as the snow melted it created a wall of snow. That was where they lived. It was bad staying in the open air, day and night but what was even worse was that they didn't have one basic necessity: no food and no means of getting it.

David Berg, who had found refuge with a farmer with whom he had a special relationship, took food up to them every few days weather permitting. He continued to do so until signs of spring began to emerge. David really went out of his way to supply those guys with food and some clothing that he was able to get from the farmer. He deserves a lot of credit for having done what he did. There weren't too many of us who volunteered to do it. It was a big undertaking and commitment on his part.

Some of us went back to the bunker. After we fled and the Germans reached the bunker, they threw in a few grenades and destroyed it including our precious hand-mill, which was smashed into a thousand pieces. This was a great loss. Where we last saw him firing from behind a tree at the Germans, we found David Laufer's body. A German machine gun took him out. He was lying alongside the tree and his head had been blown off. He paid the supreme price and without his sacrifice most of us would not be alive.

Next to the bunker we found the body of Yankel the shoemaker. I learned that Yankel and Avrum Berg stayed outside in the open for a few days in another place in the forest and then decided to return to the bunker thinking that the Germans wouldn't return having just attacked it. It seems that Yankel and Avrum weren't very careful. They had a fire going continuously because they were cold, but one of the farmers spotted the smoke, as faint as it may have been, and notified the Germans. Naturally the Germans responded. They found the two "criminals". They killed Yankel immediately on the spot, but the Germans decided to question Avrum Berg. They kept their prisoner for a few days hoping to get information out of him about the rest of us. He took the Germans on a wild goose chase, either deliberately or out of ignorance until they finally realized that Avrum didn't know where we were. They finished him off too.

We found Mrs. Schuster's pregnant body halfway up the mountain and returned it to the bunker along with Yankel's and David Laufer's. Then we covered them with rocks and soil before leaving the bunker-grave to return to our group.

As we gathered news from our various contacts, we became keenly aware that the news from the Russian front was very encouraging. In fact we knew that the Russians were approaching eastern Poland as it existed in 1939. It was late April, early May 1944, and the weather improved. Most of us, if not all, were gathered in the Plishka Forest. Spring was here and with it -- hope. We could hear the heavy guns from far away; it was music to our ears. In early evening, just as darkness set in, we would hear and sometimes see planes flying over the area on the way to Germany on bombing missions.

One day early in May 1944, Moyshe, Feiler and a few others of authority, decided to go and rob a farmer in the village of Zybryce (pronounced "ZIB-ri-tza"). We were told he had guns and valuables. At that time there were wealthy and political escapees running from the Russians, mostly Ukrainians who committed atrocities back when the war started. The Russians were putting a great deal of pressure on the Germans.

It was about the middle of May, when a group of us, about 12 to15 all together, went to Zybryce to a specific wealthy farmer to obtain guns and relieve him of some valuables. Zybryce was north of where we were hiding and over several high mountains. It was a big mistake to go there and hold up that farmer.

We used the same method as we did in our previous endeavor several months earlier before the winter started. Avrum Feiler, again with his gun, pretended we were the police and ordered the farmer to open the door. We went in, each at his own discretion, to look for whatever we could find. Feiler and Tatko tried to obtain guns, but to no avail. After a while, the guys in charge of the operation told to us clear out and we headed back to our forest hideout. We came back early in the morning. Each one of us was supposed to declare what we took. I don't think anyone declared any valuables, and if valuables were any taken, I don't think they admitted it.

Zybryce was a hostile village. That entire area north and east of the village, which extended to more villages, was inhabited by farmers as well as laborers that worked in lumber and related industries. When the war broke out in June of 1941, the inhabitants of those villages took charge of the area before the Germans moved in. They killed most of the Jews in those villages, saving the Germans the trouble. If they hadn't believed it before, they now knew there were still Jews in the area. The villagers of Zybryce, with the help of the local foresters, decided to search and to find us.

Less than a week later I was back at my routine of food gathering. The night May 20th, I was in my village, Radycz, to get some food. It was a bright night with pleasant temperature and I struck out for camp carrying the food on my back. It must have been about 3 or 4a.m. I had walked this way many, many times before, always on guard, always with fear but without incident. When I returned there were a few guys sitting around. A couple of them were playing cards; a small fire was the only source of light. I lingered on for a time watching the card players before I went to lie down and get some sleep.

Mordche Weicher was up. He walked away from the fire about 50 feet, probably to get some twigs for the fire, but heard some movement in the distance. He came back to where we were sitting and before he could complete a sentence, shots rang out from one side of the camp. We scattered, running in the opposite direction. Schuster fell heavily to the ground, shot and killed on the spot by our assailants.

Confused and frightened, we ran down and across the mountain wall and the valley to the next wall, not knowing where to go and what to expect. I ran and then slowed down afraid of my own shadow. I stopped and listened, then ran on, not really knowing what to do.

They found us on May 21, 1944, and I knew that I must have been watched as I returned from Radycz. I hadn't realized that I was being watched. As careful as I had been, I walked all the way back to camp without being aware of anything in any way. Those individuals that were watching me could have very easily caught me without any trouble, but instead they let me pass so that I could lead them to the group. That's what they were after, not just one individual.

No one chased us into the mountains and we wandered looking for others who had escaped. In the afternoon, I ran into Moyshe and then my uncle Srul and then a few others. The next day the rest of us found each other in a place where we had stayed before in the Plishka Forest. This was a better place because it was closer to the friendly village; the wall of the forested mountain was steeper, the trees were shorter and much denser. We were all back together except for Schuster.

It was an irony of life: right after David Laufer and Schuster's wife were killed at the bunker, Bronia, Laufer's girlfriend became Schuster's girlfriend and of course that relationship ended abruptly when Schuster was killed. You might be thinking "how could Schuster and Bronia hook up after just having their loved ones killed in cold blood?" Right? Well, even though this is so hard to explain, our emotions were completely frozen. Our conscience was numb. We didn't think whether things were right or wrong, because anyone of us could be killed the next moment.

What do we do now? We were all very frightened at this point. The robbery in Zybryce was definitely a huge mistake and we expected the worst. The local people from Zybryce, with the help of foresters who found us a week or so ago, might expand their search and try to find us again. Some of us, particularly those from the Sambor Ghetto that joined us last year, were adamant to abandon our place in Plishka and move to a forest called Zymna Hora (pronounced "ZIM-na HO-ra...which means "cold mountain"). Some of us were somewhat less pessimistic and wanted to stay in Plishka Forest reasoning that we knew the area better, as well as the friendly farmers in the village that were helping us all along. Zymna Hora, on the other hand, is farther away without any or very few farmers that would help. The discussions went on and on but, ultimately, we decided to split.

All of the people that came to us from the Sambor Ghetto decided to move to the Zymna Hora. Moyshe, Srul and I, as well as David Berg and Elka along with a few others decided to join that Zymna Hora group. They had the guns. In total, there were about five or six, but our supply of ammunition was woefully small, perhaps each had approximately seven or eight bullets. This was hardly enough for any fight or confrontation, but enough to make a name for ourselves and prove that the Jews were armed; certainly a deterrent for someone trying any monkey business.

One night before moving, Feiler, Binder, Tatko Liebhart, Itzik Operman and I went to the Zymna Hora and found a suitable place to relocate. I went with them, even though I was younger, because I knew the area much better, especially leading from the Plishka to the Zymna Hora. We had to cross my village of Radycz and I knew some friendly farmers -- the others didn't.

On the way back from the Zymna Hora to the Plishka we again had to cross my village. I was going to see one of the farmers to get some food. I instructed the other four to sit very quietly at the farmer's orchard outside the house. The next farm was very close by. It would be easy to arouse the farmer if they made any noise.

It was around 1 or 2 a.m. when I went to the farm house. I was inside putting together food to bring back with me, when I heard gunfire, two shots. I ran out of the house from the opposite side running away from the sound of firing. I didn't know what was going on. Gunfire was never good. Where were my companions? Had they been caught? Killed? Who was after us? I ran.

I ran up the mountain until I reached the higher slopes. Then, I waited. I knew the point where my friends would have to pass in order to get back to the group. Sure enough, after a little while, I began to see men coming up the mountain. Finally, I recognized the guys and we were reunited. Then they told me the story.

One of the guys, not paying attention to my instructions decided to pick an apple from the tree. This noise from the tree aroused the adjacent farmer who came out of the house to investigate. The farmers were usually dressed in white linen slacks and nightshirt when they went to sleep. One of the four guys became frightened to see the individual dressed in white, panicked and fired a shot, which was very unusual. One of the other guys, not knowing who fired, returned the fire, creating a frightening moment in the immediate neighborhood. This could've been a set up and we all could've been killed -- all for an apple.

It was really ridiculous, but I believe that being scared most of the time is what helped keep me alive. It was the kind of fear that steeled my will to survive. Maybe it was the idea that I was too close to surviving the horrors all around us for so long, surviving a war we were fighting here in our mountains, surviving the constant fear of being discovered – all to get killed for an apple. Yes, it was ridiculous, but I wasn't laughing.

11

The Tents in Zymna Hora

This is how we walked, with death hovering over us at all times. In spite of it all, we went on and did what we had to do. We fought back whichever way we could, even though the odds were against us in a big way. We longed to live to see the defeat of the Nazis as well as their sympathizers and friends. We know that the day of their defeat is not too far away and that we have to make it for our sake and for the sake of all those that couldn't and didn't make it.

We moved to Zymna Hora to a spot in the middle of the forest wall with trees that protected us in case anyone tried to find us. Even though we moved to a new place, the danger of discovery followed us wherever we went. The best that we could do was to make our discovery as difficult as possible for our enemies – and there were many. As always, we had someone standing guard at all times to warn us of anything or any unusual sound. Our time in hiding had not diminished our caution. Quiet the contrary, it had sharpened it.

The top of our mountain was the highest peak in the area. From there we could see for miles over the entire area; it was a panorama. For two months, July and August, we lived in makeshift tents -- three to five people to a tent -- depending on the group. How many people to a tent, depended on the relationships among them. Before, all the activities started with the German pullback, we didn't spent any time on the top of the mountain. We would stay in the middle of the mountain wall, trying to be as inconspicuous as possible.

Then the day came when we began to believe that there was no doubt that the Russians were pursuing the Germans in a big way. In the morning, all of us went up to the mountain peak and watched the activities of the day. The Russian planes we saw flying over had large red stars and were often firing their machine guns. Once, the Germans shot down a Russian plane a few villages away. We saw German armor, trucks and all sorts of vehicles moving south and west towards Germany. With each passing day the activities increased and we watched with great satisfaction and jubilation. We could smell the day of liberation, and yet we couldn't help but remember that we were still under a death sentence.

In order to get food we went down to the village with Shulim Erdman who used to live there. Food became scarce, so we decided to steal a calf. As soon as we caught the calf we took it into the forest to our camp. Fresh meat was a treasure and I felt much stronger after a hearty meal filled with protein.

One day, it must have been mid-July 1944, we were sitting around, discussing politics, past and present and speculating about the future. Our guard suddenly appeared and told us that someone was approaching the camp. This alerted the guys with the guns. The stranger got closer and closer. As soon as he was close enough, we surrounded and caught him.

He was one of the Ukrainian Nationalists who was looking for one of those Ukrainian Nationalist groups that had sprung up to fight the Germans, the Russians and any Jews they found. A Ukrainian Nationalist was not welcome in our midst but we listened to his story without betraying our feelings.

The young Ukrainian guy, about 20 years old, was very pleased to have found us. He was under the mistaken impression that we were the group he was looking for. We were dressed just like the local populace; most of us spoke Ukrainian like any native, except those who lived in town Turka. Those Jews spoke mostly Yiddish and had an accent when they spoke Ukrainian so they said nothing.

The young guy chattered away and didn't have nice words to say about the Jews. Then, slowly he began to realize that he might be in the wrong hands. He went pale and went quiet.

"What do we do with him?" A small group including Avrum Feiler, Moyshe Hans, David Binder, and Tatko Liebhart got together to decide what to do. We knew we couldn't let him go because he knows where we are and he will bring his friends back to kill us. There was no way we could keep him captive under our living conditions. It wasn't practical. There was only one solution and the group decided—we must kill him.

"Any volunteers to do the job?" asked Feiler.

One of the original members of our group who came from the Sambor Ghetto, Benciyon Bernanke, volunteered. Benciyon Bernanke, the good looking ladies man, always preening, walking around trying to act like a tough guy, was going to execute our Ukrainian enemy. That was a surprise. In reality, he was a lot of hot air and avoided going to places where it was too dangerous. However, he volunteered to do the job and, almost predictably, screwed it up. David Binder gave him the loaded revolver. He aimed at the frightened guy's head and fired. Instead of going into the Ukrainian's head, the bullet went into his cheek on one side and came out on the other. The guy screamed; he could be heard for miles. David Binder finished the job and killed the guy. It wasn't the way we wanted it, but it had to be done if we wanted to survive.

Several weeks later, two Hungarian soldiers came upon us unexpectedly, much to our surprise. Those of us with guns surrounded them. The soldiers did nothing; they just gave up. One of the soldiers spoke only Hungarian; the other spoke a little German. Communicating with them was not easy. They told us that they were guarding Hungarian Jews in a labor camp in Turka. We didn't understand exactly how they got this far to reach us. At any rate, here they were.

They realized that we were Jews. We found ourselves in another dilemma; similar to that with the Ukrainian Nationalist we did away with several weeks earlier. But this was much more difficult.

What to do with these two Hungarian soldiers? Again we reconvened the "high tribunal" to discuss this matter. On the one hand, if we kill them we could have their rifles that we desperately need; we would not have to worry that they would report us or tell anyone. Perhaps we should bribe them, trust them and hope for the best.

On the other hand, if we kill them, we may invite a big problem, bigger than we could handle. Half of the police and the Hungarian contingent could be looking for them and indirectly for us. We could jeopardize our survival. We are so close to victory and survival and yet so far.

We spoke to them in a very limited way because of the language barrier. They came across as very understanding, sympathetic and as "friends". They said they were very nice to the Jews as guards and were opposed to what was being done to the Jews. What else would or could they say under the circumstances. They knew very well that their lives were in our hands. A decision, however, had to be made as difficult as it was to let them go or kill them. There was no shortage of guys who would volunteer to carry out the execution.

It wasn't an easy decision and as risky as it was the decision was made to bribe them and let them go. Of course, they weren't in a good bargaining position; they knew it and we knew it. Nevertheless, the "elders" were persuaded that letting them go was the more prudent thing to do. I don't know whose watch it was but someone volunteered to make the contribution. We gave them the watch and the soldiers promised to keep our existence a secret.

Just as a precaution, we moved away from this camp to another well-forested area nearby and kept extra vigilance for the next week or two. No one came looking for us and we believed that the Hungarian soldiers had kept their promise.

The war activities intensified. We lived during the night in the middle of the mountain wall. In the morning we would move to the mountain peak, which was bare and where the view was spectacularly unlimited. We could see the German armor moving south and hear the artillery exchanges in the distance. Everyone was very tense; we didn't know what to expect, but we liked what we saw and all of us spent a lot of time on top of the mountain.

Some problems were of our own making. Most of us realized that every moment that we let our guard down might bring peril near us. Sometimes things barely noticed under normal circumstances became magnified by the danger all around us. A few drinks might make you do something silly or at the worst get you arrested but on this occasion the results were life-threatening. Back in October of last year, Itzik Eimer and Schuster went down to the village and brought back some whiskey. With such a precious acquisition, they celebrated by drinking all the way back to the camp becoming slightly inebriated by the time they arrived. That night, the whiskey dulled their brains but sharpened their other appetites and soon it was apparent that both Schuster's wife and Eimer's girlfriend were pregnant.

The Germans had killed Schuster's pregnant wife in the March attack. But Sally, Itzik Eimer's pregnant girlfriend, was due to give birth any day. Rumor had it, perhaps any minute.

Our concern was unspoken but I thought that a baby living with our group in the forest would be difficult, if not impossible. I had no idea what Eimer or Sally planned to do. Certainly, Sally would have to risk discovery and find shelter in the village. Even that seemed impossible. She knew where we were. We would not be safe if she was caught. That was not an option. I wasn't the only one trying to work out the solution to this problem.

During the day, more and more Russian planes flew over the territories as well as at night. They frequently came quite near but we were sheltered deep in the forest and watched without fear. In fact, watching the planes gave us confidence. Soon, we hoped, we would be leaving the forest to begin living like free men.

One evening in late July 1944, we were sitting around the fire where we cooked. It was isolated and covered from the sides so as to make the flames invisible. Of course, we could not cover the top, nor did we expect any problems from "heaven". We heard a plane flying over, which was not uncommon at this point. There was a sudden burst of machine gun fire from above. The ground around the fire erupted as the shells aimed at our fire struck, ripping through the trees and the leaves above us.

We threw water and everything else available on the fire dousing the immediate target. Elke, Alis and Blime ran about but not because of the attack. They were looking for towels and cloths for Sally who was in labor. Everything seemed chaotic. No one was hit in the attack but it was apparent that the Russian plane had fired at the flames without any knowledge of us or anyone else. It was just a good target. A few minutes later, we all heard the cry of a baby. It was Sally's baby. "What should we do?" We could no longer put off that question.

Everyone joined in the discussion with our council regarding the baby. We were practically on the front lines. We knew the Germans were retreating, but where will they take a stand and fight? When will it happen? It could take a few days or perhaps a few weeks. Could we have one baby jeopardizing the entire group of 35 people? We would all be in danger. The council made the decision -- *we can't keep the baby*.

They spoke to Itzik Eimer and told him that since it was his baby, he was responsible for getting rid of the baby. It was his decision as to how he was going to do it. In the morning, needless to say, there was no baby. No one knew what he did or how he did it. There were rumors whispered that Itzik choked his own child. But because of the sensitivity, no one ever mentioned it again. As I mentioned earlier, life had very little meaning (even though one's own survival had immense meaning). And even the unimaginable thought of killing your own child, had little emotion attached to it because we did what we had to do.

It was getting very difficult to get food. We were not as close to the farmers where we used to stay before we moved to Zymna Hora. The guys from Turka with the help of Shulim Erdman who used to live in the village of Yavor, "negotiated" with a farmer and brought back a calf which satisfied our hunger for a while.

Life went on; we were spending more and more time on the mountain peak observing, watching with great satisfaction all the activities on the roads. There was no mistake. The Germans were moving out.

Early one morning in the first week of August 1944, we finished eating what we called breakfast and wasted no time getting back up to the mountain peak to see what was going on. We were fascinated with our vantage point watching what we thought of as our freedom being fought out in the distance.

Every day, we climbed upward from where we slept and cooked our meals through the forest to where only thick bushes covered the mountainside. The last 15 feet of the mountain was bare. It was not a large area but the view was breathtaking for many reasons. The most important was the sight of Germans departing. We all wished them the best in Hell.

As we were sitting enjoying the view, trying not to call any attention to ourselves, we noticed figures on the smaller mountain peak to the south of us. We counted 12 figures walking single file along a mountain ridge. They were about a mile or a mile and a half away heading towards us. We realized that it was a German patrol. We had a much higher and better observation point. We got the message loud and clear; they wanted our mountain peak. I don't think they saw us but we ran as fast as we could down our mountain. Everyone reached the bottom except Hillel Erdman.

No one had seen Hillel up on the peak. He had been asleep when we left camp. No one woke him but we assumed that he would follow later. Hillel was missing but we couldn't look for him. We stayed at the foot of the mountain the rest of the day and early in the evening he found us there.

Hillel said that we were gone when he finally woke up. He assumed that the entire group had gone up to the top of the mountain, as we had for the last few weeks. He left camp and began the climb up. As Hillel reached the end of the bushes he saw Germans, a "pleasant" surprise, the unbelievable.

Immediately, he realized what was happening. The Germans said to him "K*om, kom*" which means come, come here. As he said, "I am coming", Hillel threw himself back into the bushes and ran down the mountain. The Germans fired a few futile shots but did not pursue him. Eventually he found us.

We didn't know what was happening, but the next afternoon, we heard artillery firing. It originated somewhere south of us and then we heard the explosion of the shell north of us. David Berg and a few others who served in the Polish army realized that we were caught between the German artillery and the German infantry.

Now we found ourselves in a very peculiar situation; we had not eaten anything for two days. We were afraid to make any moves. Fortunately for us, at this juncture there were also farmers in the forest as well as on the meadows with their cattle. The Germans located a mile or so east of us were not the SS. These were frontline soldiers, combat troops. Germans on the fighting front were not actively looking for Jews in particular.

We caught a calf with the consent of a farmer—at least I believed we had his consent—slaughtered it and cut it up. David Berg was in charge of this operation, since he was a butcher in civilian life before the war.

We made a fire using only twigs, dry and thin twigs that would not generate smoke to boil the meat. We also found some coal in the vicinity left over from other fires. We were doing fairly well; the coals became hot as we blew on them to keep them hot. We had some potatoes that we dug up in the fields. At this time of the year, potatoes were available in the fields owned by farmers. We hadn't eaten for two and half days. We were weak and starving, but the fear and the anxiety kept us going. Finally, we began to see bubbles coming up and the potatoes began to boil as well as the meat. Just another 15 to 20 minutes and we will eat. The taste was forming in my mouth.

As all of us salivated for the food, we looked up. There was a German patrol, three soldiers standing above us about 50 yards away, yelling in German, *"Was Fleisch?"* What, meat?

Seeing those Germans was like seeing the angels of death and we all ran away in the opposite direction. There were farmers working in the fields but no one bothered us; they were concerned about their own safety. That was probably the first time we ran through part of the village in daytime. As fast as we could we darted into the forest and stayed there until it got dark. At night, some of us crept back to the place where we cooked the meat. We noticed that the Germans had been there and helped themselves to some of the meat, but left most of it. We were glad to get the meat and carried it back to camp. Those carrying the meat helped themselves in a big way but some of it reached the group.

I had the feeling that either we are invisible or God is working a miracle and watching over us. The only question was where was God before when we needed him desperately? Not that we don't need him now. Being caught between the German artillery and its infantry made it almost impossible to function. The German military uniform is enough to make me faint and I do not exaggerate.

There were no options. Two houses in the area were isolated from the main village. We used to visit those farmers on several occasions before the Germans showed up in the area. Now it was much more difficult to maneuver around. Because of that, food was scarce as was our safety and existence. Where do we go? What do we do? The Russians are only a mountain or two away. We can almost touch the freedom and yet...

We knew now that before the German patrol occupied the top of the mountain where we stayed, the Russians were just north of our position. If we had known that then, instead of running down the mountain in the southern direction, had we just changed directions and run north to the next mountain, we would have reached the Soviet Army before the Germans took up positions. But who knew?

A few days later, things settled down somewhat. Planes still roamed the sky and we could hear artillery fire as well as machine gun fire but around us things were otherwise relatively quiet. In the evening we would crawl down to the farm, making sure that the Germans were not around. We tried to get some food and find out what was happening, not that the farmer knew much more than we did.

We definitely needed a safer place where the Germans and the farmers with their cattle don't roam around freely. There was another mountain close by. Large trees and rocks covered the extremely steep north westerly side of that mountain. It was so steep that is was almost suitable for professional mountain climbers. For our purposes, it was really inaccessible to friend or foe. Several of the guys went there to explore it and found out that it was probably the best place to stay at the present time. Around the end of August 1944, we all moved to that God-forsaken place. It was steep and hard to move around, but it felt a great deal safer. From this place we could see pretty far out. On the right, flatland extended around a poor farmer's place all along to the north until it reached the next mountain. We used to visit that farmer in the weeks past, but now it is "*verboten*". There were Germans moving openly around in the vicinity. A few days later three or four pieces of field artillery moved into the area. From where we were, we could see the Germans manning the guns; we could also see the woman on the farm bringing some food to the Germans voluntarily or otherwise. It was an eerie feeling being so close to the Germans.

The weather was good and that was very helpful to us. The visibility was almost unlimited. We were looking out from the dense trees and bushes without anyone seeing us. Everyone was very anxious, every minute counted. We talked about what was happening, what could happen, what might happen, all a great deal of speculation. Every one seemed to be an expert in political and military strategies. Those were exciting times as well as very apprehensive—everyone had butterflies in their stomachs.

One of our big concerns at the time was what if both sides dig in for a considerable amount of time. That would spell disaster for us. Even worse, what if cold weather was to set in? That was unthinkable.

With each passing day the people in the group were getting more and more jittery.

12

The Final Hurdle to Liberation

There was good cause for our jitters. As the Russian Army pounded away at the Germans giving us reason to cheer, the Germans fell back into an area—our area, where they had not been concentrated before. They were running out of room. That was not something to cheer about. In fact, it made our life much more dangerous.

We never knew where the Germans were going to turn up next. It was logical that they took over our fine observation point on the mountain peak. We certainly had watched their maneuvers from its vantage. Just as the mountains offered us places to hide, they also gave the Germans the same opportunity.

If we were to survive these perilous weeks or months without being surprised in our camp by German soldiers, we needed more information. Where were they? Were they likely to move into our mountain refuge in the forests?

Our best information came from the local farmers as always. Here in Zymna Hora we were farther away from the friendly Ukrainians in our own villages. We did have limited contact with local farmers. One or two of them lived at the edge of the forest where Germans were not generally present, but one never knew. We had to be cautious. Some of the farmers were in the forest with their cattle trying to keep them from falling into German hands. That was helpful.

From our few contacts, we found out that the Russians were closer than we originally thought. Some of the guys in the group talked about crossing over the river at some point to reach the Russians. It was very tempting, but also extremely dangerous. We did get some good information that there was a man in the village who knew that area and had knowledge of the movement of the Germans. That was valuable. An even more critical piece of news for those who wanted to go over to the Russians was this man's knowledge of the best place to cross over.

We debated the pros and cons. Looking for a safe place to cross was using the word safe, loosely. There was no safe place but they wanted to trust their newly-found maven, the man who knows the safest place to cross the river. Most of these people were from Turka and Sambor. Perhaps they felt less at home whereas we knew the people in our villages. So many had helped us at great risk to themselves. The remaining people, including me, decided not to chance the river crossing, but rather go back to the Plishka Forest. We wanted to rejoin the small group that remained there when we moved to Zymna Hora.

We felt that it would be safer to go back to the Plishka Forest rather than stay here in Zymna Hora where the Germans are all around us. Those in our group who decided to go back to Plishka had to make a decision. What is the best way to do it, and how to do it? I was tempted to join those who wanted to cross over to the Soviet side. On the other hand, I felt that we would be better off going back to Plishka somehow and joining the others, perhaps a more conservative decision and less risky.

To accomplish this, we had to cross two villages, Losinic (pronounced: LO-si-nitz) and Ilnik. I knew Ilnik well. That was where I had gone after my family failed to return from the barracks in Turka. It was also the home of my uncle and some of our group. Ilnik was an unusual village. It was made up of groups of houses and farms strung out along the river. Unlike most villages where the houses clustered around a crossroad or central point, Ilnik was divided by not only by the river Stryj (pronounced: STRAY) but also by its tributaries flowing down from the mountains. The part of Ilnik we had to cross was near my village Radycz.

Losinic was quite different. It was in an area with little forest cover and bare mountains, not too high but dangerous. There were Germans in the villages, especially in Losinic. This is the ground we had to cover until we finally reached the Plishka Forest.

Perhaps the idea was crazy, but just as crazy was crossing the river to the Soviet side. We knew one thing -- we couldn't stay where we were. Food was very scarce; it wasn't easy to approach the local farmers. Time was not on our side, especially if the weather worsened.

Reluctantly, we decided to take the plunge. There was always danger when we moved from one place to another. We thought it would be a good idea to send Elke and Blime, dressed like Ukrainian girls, with a farmer's wife who could explain they were her daughters or nieces in case they were stopped. They left us in the middle of the day when women walking in the area would be less suspicious. The Germans, as a rule, didn't bother women, unless the woman was attractive, then the Germans would force her to have sex. By now the morale of the Germans was pretty low. They didn't bother the local population unless they needed something, then all hell would break loose. The Germans looked at the locals with disdain and arrogance – as if they were subhuman.

We waited to hear if Elke and Blime had made the journey safely. A message came back through the farmer that they made it successfully. That was a relief and encouraged those of us waiting to make a similar journey.

Late one evening in mid-September 1944, we decided to go. It may not have been the best time because it was a clear sky with almost a full moon. We felt we had to leave.

David Berg took his World War I rifle. Why? I didn't know; it was absurd. It was barely operational. It didn't make any sense to bring it because all it could have done was get us into deeper trouble, especially if caught.

We went up the hill where there were German artillery guns. We were very careful while bypassing the Germans manning the guns. In the clear bright evening we moved as quietly as possible. Then we had to descend into Losinic, cross a small stream and move up into the mountain. We were crossing the stream and the village's only road when we heard Germans in the nearby farmhouse.

I froze. We tried to see what was happening. I felt numb, as if I was in a make-believe world. I didn't believe this was happening. Hiding in the bushes, we saw an area where the houses were not close together that would be a good spot to cross. We couldn't stay; we had to move fast. We started past the farmhouses. Somehow David Berg lost his old rifle. Stubbornly, he started to look for it. Time was not our friend. Any moment someone might see us.

Just as I wanted to pull him along, David found his rifle. We passed between the farmhouses, staying as low as possible. We heard men talking loudly in German but we couldn't make out what they said. Occasionally a horse would snort loudly. It struck the nerves.

Past the houses, we crossed the village and were on the way up the mountainside where we would cross over to the next village on the way to Plishka. A few times a flare shot into the sky, popped into a bright glow, lighting the road or a field, then burning out as it fell. That was the way an army detected any movement. David Berg told us to lie down and freeze.

As we walked uphill we tried to stay close to the bushes wherever possible. Near the top of the hill, tiny lights surrounded us. At first we were scared not knowing what it was. Finally we realized that they were fireflies. For one moment we were walking through millions of darting, flickering insects.

A thought went through my mind. We were in the middle of the most crucial time, the most dangerous, the most vulnerable, the most unpredictable time. Should we have gone over to the Russians? God forbid anything should happen; we've spent almost 23 months staying alive—waiting to be liberated. We could almost touch it and yet the whole thing could come to an abrupt end—right now, here in a field of lights. While my mind was thinking what could happen, in my heart, I was sure that we would make it. This conviction had followed me throughout my hiding; I had no explanation for it.

Some of the tension, the fear, was relieved because we were on our way to Plishka, a more comfortable place in terms of security. I knew that place much better. Most importantly, it was removed from the center where it could turn out to be a battlefield. Another hour or perhaps an hour and a half and we would be there. Perhaps we would find the other part of the group that decided not to join us in Zymna Hora several months ago.

We crossed the top of the mountain and started down the mountain into Radycz, the second village, hoping not to encounter any Germans. We moved carefully and quietly, taking our time, listening and keeping aware of possible dangers. I knew the area well. This was my home turf.

This was where I walked as a very little boy to the school in Ilnik from our village.

I felt a surge of hope being so near my home. We crossed the small river in an area where there were no farmhouses, just land. We were then on our final step of the journey to the Plishka, up the mountain covered with small trees. I had the feeling that when we reach the thickly forested area, we will be close to our Promised Land and safety. Fortunately for us, we had not seen or heard anything menacing after crossing the second mountain. Although we had not been in this area for several months, I felt safer here. There seemed to be little change; then as we got closer to Plishka we encountered telephone wires. A chill went through my spine. Crossing over the wires, we hurried to reach the trees at the edge of the forest.

We were finally in the Plishka. Now it was just a question of going up the mountain to the area where we stayed before Zymna Hora. This was home. The people who stayed should be in an area not far from where we were, but it was pitch dark in the trees. It was almost impossible to see, almost like going blind. When we finally reached the area where we thought they should be, we decided that the best thing to do is to sit down and wait for any signs. We knew the tricks of the trade, what to listen for: noise of a dish, a walk, last glow of a fire about to die.

Everyone sat quietly, listening. After a while, we heard a faint noise coming from one direction. We moved very cautiously toward it. Then we saw a blink of a faint fire and as we came even closer, we saw someone taking a few steps. It was Mordche Weicher. Mordche was the kind of a guy that would always snoop around the perimeter. Naturally, we didn't want him to hear us in any way. Just hearing something out in the blackness of the forest was frightening enough. We all knew that terrible feeling. Knowing someone was hiding outside the camp area and watching was terrifying, especially not knowing who it was. Nevertheless, we had to make contact and let them know that we were there. Moyshe called Mordche and identified himself as we all joined in.

It was a relief to hear that nothing much has been happening, except for occasional firings. Of course, we had long stories to tell each other, and we did.

Everyone wondered what was going to happen. How long will this last? Something has to give, but when? Food was scarce. We were frightened to go anywhere. This wasn't the time to be exposed in any shape or form and risk our lives unnecessarily.

On very few occasions, we would venture into the fields to dig for potatoes, carrots and anything else ready to eat. A few times we went down to the edge of the forest to two farmhouses and tried to obtain some food. Most of the time we just waited and enjoyed the planes flying over on the way to the west to release their bombs on German industry or whatever they were bombing. We sat around full of hope and yet a lot of apprehension. We had been on the front, on the wrong side unfortunately, for almost two and half months.

September came with its deteriorating weather. That was always a worry, especially now when we were so short of food and our ragged clothes might not make it through another winter. Winter, the cold weather could be setting in at any time. This could present a very serious problem for us. It was almost unthinkable. What gave us such hope and inspired us was the sound of artillery bombardment, machine gun firing but mostly airplanes flying west. We always wondered why we didn't hear or see the planes returning east. They must have been returning by a different route; that was our interpretation.

Just as the nights began to grow colder and we began to despair that we would not survive another winter, everything changed. Suddenly, on September 24th, a big battle broke out about 20-30 miles to the west of us. It was intense, lasting all night until about five in the morning. We heard heavy artillery and big explosions, back and forth. And then, as suddenly as it started, it stopped. A complete calm permeated the entire area, as if everything stopped dead.

We all became experts. No one really had any experience to explain the stillness except for David Berg who had a short tour in the Polish-German war, which was over as soon as it started, the Poles being defeated within a few days by the super race. However, David did have a lot of advice and sounded like a real expert on the theater of operation. One didn't have to be a big maven to realize that something very serious happened as a result of the battle that took place during the night.

Very few doubted that the Russians had broken the German-Hungarian lines. One reason was that we absolutely wanted to believe it; it was in the air; we could smell it. Of course, all things being equal, no one really knew for sure. Our hope was high and no one had the patience to wait until dawn. We thought daylight would show us some tangible evidence that the Russians had broken through and that the Germans were on the run. What a thought that was! It was a dream come true after four long years, two of those on death row.

Dawn came so slowly, almost teasing us. We couldn't see anything of the battle zone from our situation on the opposite side of the mountain. A number of us dared to go up the mountain hoping to get a better view of the battle area. What had happened? We didn't know. I was anxious as were my companions but when we reached the other side, the villages and beyond were quiet; there was really nothing to see. We didn't have any field glasses, but even if we had they probably could not have helped much.

Finally, daylight. Not knowing what was happening made everyone extremely nervous. Hard to believe, that we could finally be free. Srul and Moyshe decided to investigate by going to two farmhouses we often visited very close the edge of the forest. They hoped to find out what was happening. They left about seven in the morning. All of us eagerly awaited their return, but we heard nothing and we saw nothing. By eleven they had been gone for about four hours. All sorts of thoughts were going through our minds. We began to worry about the well being of our two investigators.

Isaac Weicher and I decided to look into the situation on our own. We followed the same route as did Moyshe and Srul. As we reached the edge of the forest, we saw the two farmhouses with no one in sight; no activity of any kind.

When I suggested to Isaac that we go to the farmhouses to see what was happening, Isaac refused to go. He didn't want to take a chance. I really didn't blame him. But as for me, I was too eager and somehow I felt that it was reasonably safe to go. I certainly was not trying to convince Isaac to come with me. I had this feeling, a feeling that nothing would happen to me; in fact I had these types of feelings before, especially when I was, or thought I was, in a dangerous situation. I could never understand it.

I ran over to the first farmhouse very carefully. The house was abandoned, which I didn't expect. It was a spooky feeling. Then I ran over to the second house, which was about 50 feet away. The area was very quiet but I had an uneasy feeling. As I entered the house, there was a little baby crying with no parents around. I didn't know what to think.

There was a third farmhouse at the edge of the furthermost cluster of houses in the village of Ilnik. It was risky because that house was a considerable distance away, perhaps as much as 300 yards.

I just didn't think rationally, but decided to go to the third house. Curiosity got the best of me. As usual, I had a feeling that it was okay and that nothing would happen to me -- hard to explain.

I ran down the path and into the farmhouse. Opening the door in haste, I found the couple who owned the house. Our farm was not far from them and they knew my family. They were very friendly and immediately told me that Srul and Moyshe were there about two hours before; they shaved, cleaned themselves up and went to the Ilnik to meet the Russians. Goose pimples rose all over my body. The Russians had moved in during the night.

I didn't know how to react. It couldn't be true; but it was. I took a deep breath. I was obviously pleased but I didn't feel overjoyed. I should have been, after all; I was just released from death row. I was free, but not completely. My body, my feelings began to thaw. Suddenly, a different feeling overwhelmed me. It was as if I was asking myself after two years, "who am I, what am I?" A heavy burden settled on me. I am alone. Where is my family? It was almost, as if it was not real.

I longed for my mother whom I loved dearly. She was so proud of me. But she was gone. I didn't even know where and how. My brain pieced together all that I had learned about Turka, Sambor and Belzec, creating a terrible picture. A painful thought went through my mind; how my mother felt when she was on that train, a cattle train bound for death -- her pain, her hopelessness, her helplessness, the suffering until and when she met death. Tears welled up in my eyes. I should've been full of joy at my freedom but I was full of sadness. Yes, I was free, I had survived but my mother wasn't there to share anything with me. I couldn't get over it.

And I never did.

As I sobered up a bit, and I realized that I must go back to Isaac and, the rest of the group. They didn't know that the Russians are in the village and that we are free.

We both ran up the mountain to share the news with everyone in the group. Srul and Moyshe weren't back yet. When they finally showed up, everyone in the group was angry with them for being so insensitive and irresponsible. At this point they didn't care.

Every one in the group now knew the score and started to cry, reflecting on what happened. It must've been the same kind of feeling I pondered over an hour or so before. Our feelings were frozen for the duration of the war. That was attributable to humiliation of the worst order, unimaginable fear, hunger and any other misery one can find in the dictionary. Many of the miseries aren't in the dictionary because there are no words for them.

We took our belongings (you might say our net worth) consisting of old dilapidated *shmates*, also known as old worn out cloth, and began to walk out of the forest and finally down into the village. A village that none of us had seen in daylight for twenty-three long months.

We crossed the river over a footbridge (the same river we crossed 23 months ago when we went into hiding) and reached the main street, the only street, more like the center of the village Ilnik. David Berg's empty house was close by.

In the center of Ilnik, a group of farmers came to greet us. Many of them weren't exactly pleased to see us but they greeted us warmly anyway. Our group of 15 swelled into a sizable group of people as another 15 or 20 farmers gathered around. A Russian soldier with a red star on his cap came over. His dark green poncho covered his uniform so that we could not see his rank. He asked who are these people, referring to us. We didn't exactly blend in, especially the way we were dressed. He told us that our group couldn't stand there because there was a battle still raging on that mountain, pointing to the mountain south of us. "Standing there is dangerous," he said.

Then he turned to us, inquiring who we were. We, along with the farmers, told him that we were Jews; we were just liberated this morning and we told him that we spent 23 months in the forest. He wanted to know whether we were hungry; he wanted to bring us over to the field kitchen and feed us.

Of course, we were very thankful for his offer, but surprisingly, we were not hungry. We chatted with him for a while. Then he took off his poncho and introduced himself by saying, "I am Captain Zurbin and I am a Jew". To me this was an extremely emotional moment. I cried like a baby. We all cried. One Jew liberating another Jew...a moment I will never forget.

We all moved into David Berg's house. It was "*erev*" (the eve of) Yom Kippur 1944. Which I remember was September 25th.

While we stayed in David Berg's house, we watched a show, columns of German prisoners of war being led away by the Russian soldiers. It was sight to behold to see Hitler's "invincible, heroic Germans, the pure superior race" marching in defeat. We watched with great satisfaction, to say the least. Hundreds of Russian troops and transport passed by. These were not the ragged soldiers we had seen early in the war but well equipped men. No longer horse drawn wagons but real trucks, U.S trucks, rumbled along Ilnik's street. The wounded passed by in ambulances, Russian as well as Germans soldiers on their way, we imagined, for medical treatment.

Our war was over. I should've been very happy; after all, this was what I longed for all these months. Yet, the feeling, the enthusiasm, the desire I had to see the end of the war suddenly became clouded by that feeling of emptiness. My family was gone forever. My heart ached. The landscape was the same but the view had taken on a different meaning. I knew I couldn't stay here. This land -- the villages, the farms, even the river -- would be constant reminders of what I had lost—all that was so very dear to me. I decided that eventually I would end up in Palestine or America or anywhere for that matter, just out of this cursed land and far away from the horrors that I was forced to endure as a young kid.

On September 26th, 1944, I started a new life.

Epilogue

Our entire group came out from the forest as well as a few who managed to survive hidden by farmers. There were other survivors who returned from the Soviet Union. For safety reasons, we all stayed in Turka. It was much too dangerous to venture out into the villages. Some of the liberated Jews went to their villages and were killed by the locals. They may have been killed for hate reasons, but the main reason was the locals' fear that those Jews might try to reclaim property that once was theirs. Many Ukrainians took over empty properties believing that the area was truly *Judenfrei*.

We heard of instances where Jewish parents, believing that their chances of survival as a family were unlikely, placed their young children with gentiles to save the children's' lives.

In one such instance a little girl, six or seven years old, named Esther was reclaimed from a farmer, not by Esther's parents but by a survivor Itzik-Moyshe Schwartz who survived hidden by a farmer. Itzik-Moyshe was a friend of Esther's parents and knew what had happened to Esther. At first the farmer refused to give her up. She was a beautiful and smart little girl. Finally the farmer returned the child. I recall little Esther wasn't too happy to be uprooted from the home she had accepted as her own. She wanted to go to church; crossed her heart every morning, the way she learned at the farmer's house. Rose Breitbart, the daughter of Itzik-Moyshe, told me that Avrum Feiler happened to be in their house and sang "*Mein Yiddishe Mame*", *My Jewish Mother*, a well known song. Suddenly, it evoked something in Esther's mind; she remembered that song from her earlier childhood with her parents and other memories came back to her. Not all children found their way back into the Jewish

127

community. Many such children were never found because there was no one to claim them.

Though it was over for us, the war continued as the Soviets drove the Germans back to the gates of Warsaw. There they waited out the winter before renewing their assault on Germany itself. While the war was still going on, everyone found a place to stay in Turka in Jewish houses abandoned during the awful days of 1942. As yet they had not been claimed by anyone. For us it was a godsend but also a tragic reminder of what the once thriving Jewish community had lost.

Everyone had some sort of a job. Moyshe Hans was instrumental in securing jobs at the lumber industry for most of the people. I worked as a clerk for Captain Zurbin, the same captain who, on the day of liberation, introduced himself by saying, "I am also a Jew". He was in charge of an induction office, inducting able men into the army and needed help in his office. He wanted someone who could write, fill out forms, prepare schedules and perform other clerical duties. I fit the bill and had the added advantage of fluency in Ukrainian, Polish and German.

All of us were biding our time, waiting for the war to end. We talked about getting out of this cursed God-forsaken place. No one had any thoughts of remaining in Turka, with two exceptions. Itzik Operman fell in love with a Russian girl and had no intention of going anywhere. Srul Singer, who stayed in Ilnik, was going to marry the woman who helped him survive during the war.

When the war ended on May 8, 1945, every one began to think how he could get out of the area as soon as possible. Fortunately, the Soviets had arranged procedures to permit Polish citizens in the Ukraine to move to Poland, now that Russia was annexing the country's pre-war eastern territories. During July 1945, most of the Jews left Turka forever and embarked on a journey never to return.

All of those who wanted to emigrate had to go to Sambor, because that is where the transports were being arranged to move to Poland. From Poland they would go to the west through Germany. The people in the Joint Distribution Committee, known as Joint or J.D.C. made procedural arrangements setting up the transports by train to Poland.

I left Sambor on just such a train with some of the people I knew from the forest including my uncle Srul. This particular transport train, consisting of freight cars, took us to Gleiwitz (pronounced: GLY-vitz) which was not far from Krakow. Eventually most of the Jews from Turka wound up in Gleiwitz or in adjacent towns. We viewed this place as a transitional point. Our intention was to go from there westward to the American Zone of Occupation. In November, a transport by freight train was arranged to take us right through East Germany, the Soviet Zone of Occupation to Munich in West Germany, the American Zone of Occupation.

During the stay in Poland the three young girls, Esther who was reclaimed by Itzik-Moyshe, along with Esthie and Chavele who were with us in the forest, were placed in an orphanage home in the town of Bielsko. Esther had two uncles in Palestine. After only a short time in the orphanage, with the help of Itzik-Moyshe, Esther was sent to Italy and then to her uncles.

There were a number of D.P. (displaced persons) camps set up in the American zone by the United Nations Relief and Rehabilitation Administration (UNRRA) to absorb the DPs or refugees. I wound up in such a DP camp, called Neu-Freiman Siedlung, in the suburbs of Munich. Some went to Fernwald, some to Landsberg and some to other DP camps.

In the DP camps, UNRRA provided us with essentials, but by and large it was food and clothing that came from the United States. Then JDC was also a major contributor to the welfare of the refugees.

At this point, I didn't know what would become of me. "Where will I go? What will I do?" I felt that life in the DP camp might be prolonged. I was in Germany and I didn't want to stay in the land of those who killed my family and tried to kill me, or live in the midst of those who had sought to impose the Final Solution.

At first I thought of immigrating to Palestine but as time went by I changed my mind. I believed that my chances of getting an education would be better in the United States. I always remembered my mother's word—education.

At first, living conditions in the DP camp were unpleasant, but in time things improved. We lived a life of uncertainty. For most people there was nothing to do; it was demoralizing. But as time passed people began to get settled and some were able to find out their destination as far as emigration was concerned. People in the camps began to date, get married, have children. Some met in camp, others survived the war together. The couples from our group who survived in the forest, David Berg and Elka, Aron Hans and Feige, Moyshe Hans and Blime, Avrum Feiler and Alis married almost immediately after liberation.

I worked as a clerk in the clothing department. One day, about a year later, one of the guys handling the inventory found a note written in English in one of the coats. He brought the note over to me in the office. I read the note which said "whoever receives this coat please write to me", signed Beverly, who lived in Ann Arbor, Michigan (I still have the note). I was very excited about the note and the fact that I was able to read it and understand it. Naturally, I wrote her a letter thanking her for the coat and received a reply. I was very pleased that she understood what I wrote in my broken English. We corresponded with each other for quite while but then somehow we stopped. It was a pleasant experience for me.

While in camp I attended the ORT school, taking a course as an electrical auto mechanic, a career I didn't pursue. I was also learning English taught to me by a German student. I applied for emigration to the United States, but that, unfortunately, looked like a long-term proposition.

With me in the DP camp, besides my uncle, was Avrum Heger, the guy who scared the hell out of us when he showed up at our bunker in the middle of the day, one day in February 1943.

I asked what had happened after he decided to hide with the farmer rather than join our group in the forest. He told me the farmer was able to get him falsified papers. At that time the Germans needed laborers to go to work in Germany. How ironic. The Germans were killing able Jewish men, and yet they were taking the Slavs and transferring them to Germany for work. Like many other Ukrainians, Heger decided to volunteer to go to Germany, obviously not as a Jew but as a Ukrainian. The problem was passing inspection. None of the Ukrainians were circumcised; the exceptions were the Jews. How convenient to identify a Jew. At the processing center for transport to Germany, the Germans needed help. When the Germans inquired who spoke German, of course Heger volunteered. There were very few, if any, among the local population in Turka that could speak German. Because he served as an interpreter when it came time for Heger to be processed, the Germans didn't ask him to undergo the inspection. Sheer luck. What helped him was the fact that he didn't look like a typical Jew; he had a reddish complexion, a Germanic look—the "pure Aryan". Secondly, by then the entire area was officially free of Jews; it had been free of Jews since 12/1/42. Heger was shipped to Germany and wound up working on a farm. There he got involved in a relationship with the farmer's daughter. Her brother was an *SS* man. Every time the son would show up on the farm, Heger would avoid him like the plague. After the war, Heger made it a point to tell them that he was a Jew.

Heger had a little grocery store in the camp and also conducted some black market activities. The main product he sold was whiskey, which was illegal. With the help of a few young guys, he sold the whiskey to US soldiers outside the camp. Next to our DP camp was an army camp. The US Army at that time was segregated; the soldiers stationed next to our camp were Afro-Americans. Every afternoon, the blonde German *freuleins* would line up in the front of the army barracks waiting for their "boyfriends". About three years later before I left Germany, there were about 40,000 babies born out of wedlock. There went Hitler's pure Aryan race. How ironic.

While in Germany, I had occasion to talk to a variety of Germans. It was amazing to learn that none of them were Nazis; none of them heard of atrocities perpetrated against people, particularly Jews. The Germans have this ability to play the innocent bystander. They were well aware of the laws promulgated by their government, the promises made by Hitler that the German people will own the world for a thousand years and the subhuman, which meant every one else, would become slaves to the Germans. But hardly any German was willing to take responsibility.

The Germans didn't like foreigners roaming their country. Whenever they got a chance, they would try to get even. On one occasion, I was the victim. I was riding a bicycle outside the camp. On the side of the road there were two jeeps parked. In each of the jeeps a GI sat with his freulein. I minded my own business and didn't pay much attention. One of the freuleins must have goaded the GI when suddenly, he took the jeep and cut me off on the road. He then got out and started beating me in the face. I didn't understand a word he was saying. He stopped when my nose started to bleed and just took off. The police never found out who it was. I wound up in the hospital for three days.

In 1948 the United States Congress passed a bill providing for the admission of 200,000 refugees. I believe this bill sped up my immigration to the United States.

On March 4, 1949, I left Bremerhaven on the army transport ship, *General Haan* bound for New York. Late afternoon on March 16, 1949, the ship docked outside of Brooklyn. We were told that we will be allowed to disembark the next day about 11a.m. I could see the lights of New York twinkling dimly. Looming in front of the city, I could see the magisterial and gigantic Statue of Liberty with her torch lit. I saw cars moving in both directions on the Belt Parkway. I stood on the deck looking at this enormous city, this country; my newly adopted country, not having the slightest notion what to expect.

I could hardly sleep all night. Everything seemed so mysterious. In the morning, the *General Haan* nudged into a berth in this incredible city, on the west side of Manhattan. I waited for the dawn to break, curious to see more and more of the city. It was a moment of intense excitement with joy and gratitude.

I had a distant cousin, Mollie Wolf, who found me through my uncle Srul. Mollie promised to pick me up from the boat. As I was walking out, I recognized her from the picture she had sent me. I sent her my picture as well so that we wouldn't miss each other.

It was March 17, 1949, and St. Patrick's Day in New York. Immediately, I was exposed to the parade with marching bands and everyone in green. There were parties and everywhere there was noise and celebration. It was overwhelming. My cousin explained to me the significance of the parade as well as the color green.

Here I was, 21 years old with no family, no money, no education to speak of, no profession, and I barely spoke English. The very first thing I did was to enroll in evening school. I started with the fourth grade but I found it to be too basic. The next evening I went to the fifth grade -- too basic. The following evening I went to an evening high school, Washington Irving Evening High School, which was set for new immigrants. My first class was English.

As I was sitting in the class I could hardly understand what the teacher was talking about. After the class I spoke to the teacher and told him about my dilemma. He asked how long had I been in the country. "About two weeks," was my reply. He told me that my ear has to get attuned to the English language and suggested that I stick around for a few weeks and then see him. The teacher was right. After a couple of weeks I began to get the gist of it all.

Besides going to school, I had to get a job and in a hurry. I went to the HIAS (Hebrew Immigration Association Service), to get some financial help. This organization was helping immigrants to get started. They gave me about $30 per week for three or four weeks. I went to an employment agency, paid a $15 fee and got myself a job as a window cleaner. The job wasn't exactly to my liking, but I couldn't be choosy. The first day, my boss took me with him and taught me the tricks of the trade. The second day he gave a few addresses where I should go to clean windows up in the Bronx. On one of the jobs, as I was cleaning the windows I heard the woman of the house talking German to another German woman. They must have married GIs after the war. I was almost embarrassed listening to their bedroom stories. They obviously didn't expect a window cleaner to understand German. On the way out I said to her in German, "*Auf wiedersehen*". She was surprised and slightly embarrassed.

On the third day, I quit the job. It was too dangerous. I was cleaning windows on the upper floors in a residential area without the benefit of a belt. I could see people from the tenth or twelfth floor looking like ants. One wrong move and I could be history; I didn't come to this country to die.

My next job was as a delivery boy. This was much better; I was close to the ground, but the pay was rather poor. Some of my friends were making much more money. One was a carpenter and one was a tailor. I said to myself, what am I a cripple? I decided to go to ORT school (Organization for Rehabilitation through Training) and try to become an operator in the clothing business. ORT was set up to assist newcomers in learning a trade. After two weeks, my instructor told me that I was ready to go and get a job. I was hesitant but she said that they may not offer you a job at the first interview or in a second interview but eventually you will land a job. Just don't be discouraged.

I went on several interviews. I didn't have to go to an employment agency for a job; there were jobs advertised on Broadway on the lower eastside of Manhattan "Operators wanted, Operators wanted" but every time I went up for an interview , they would ask if I had any experience. My honest answer was, "No, but I graduated from ORT".

The people interviewing me were not too impressed. I was frustrated, but I wasn't giving up yet. In the afternoon I changed my method, instead of saying that I was inexperienced, I said I was experienced. When asked what I did, I decided to say that I was sewing in zippers in sport jackets. I thought that would be a simple operation. In my mind, logic dictated that sewing in zippers would be a straight line, up and then down. I didn't realize that one would have to stop at the metal piece of the zipper, cross over and continue on the opposite side.

Sure enough, I got a job. The owner of the shop introduced me to the forelady who gave me several sport jackets with about five needles, put me at a sewing machine and that was it. I was to take charge from here on. I was eager to start but frightened. I did not know what I was getting myself into. Within five minutes the five needles were gone.

Either I stopped too far from the metal piece of the zipper or I would just run into it and the needle would break. The forelady realized who she was dealing with and gave me a box of 100 needles. Within a couple of hours I improved my skill.

The next day, realizing that this was piecework, I really went out to mass produce the sewing in of zippers. By the end of the day I managed to do 75 zippers. On the third day I wanted to see if I could improve it even further. Sitting across from me was an operator who was sewing in pockets in sports jackets which was a much more complicated operation. This guy was extremely fast performing his operation; he was turning out these pockets with lightning speed. I was impressed but also envious. At that point I still didn't know what they paid for sewing in zippers. I asked the guy across from me and he pointed at the wall saying that is where the price list is. Eagerly I walked over to the wall and there was the list reflecting all operations per 100. I looked for zippers and there it was. Reading across, 100 zippers 75 cents. To make sure, I read it again. Yes, it was true, 75 cents. I could not believe my own eyes. I quickly made the calculation. I may have been deficient in English but my math was okay. I worked almost two and a half days, sewed in about 200 zippers and earned a total of $1.50. Right there I decided that I would do almost anything but this.

I befriended a guy by the name of Walter in the evening high school, who told me about an opening for a position as a shipping clerk in the place where he worked. I got the job in the shipping department of Bestform Foundation and worked there for a few months. I learned a great deal about the various sizes of bras. These may have been sexy items, but after a while I found it boring; besides the pay left a lot to be desired.

All the while I had been attending evening school religiously, realizing that the only way to get somewhere is through education. In the meantime I hooked up with two guys Sishe and Leo Gleicher who came from Turka and who lived in the same rooming house where I lived. We decided to rent an apartment on the lower eastside of Manhattan, the three-room apartment was located at 242 Rivington Street. We paid about $90for the furniture. The monthly rent was nine dollars per month; my share was $3. The place was infested with hordes of cockroaches. We tried to clean it up with all sorts of methods, but nothing really seemed to work. I believe the entire block or blocks were infested with those characters. We endured for several months and then sold the furniture and gave up the "precious" apartment.

Don Hans, a brother of Moyshe Hans who was in the forest with me, introduced me to Abe Kirschner. Before he came to the United States, Kirschner knew my father during WWI. He owned Capital Flooring Corporation, a firm doing flooring installations in apartment houses. He asked me to come to see him. I told him about my job situation. He asked me if I was good in math and if I could handle the job of an estimator, explaining what the job entailed. He gave me a test and I passed, and as a result he gave me a job. In addition to being an estimator and costing out a job based on square footage, I was to answer the phone and take messages. When I heard taking messages my heart started to pound. I was frightened. I liked the set up working in an office from nine to five and he started me off with $10 more than I was making. To me this was a lot of money. Mister Kirschner had also something else in mind. He had a single daughter and thought perhaps, I could become interested in her. I took her out a few times but I had no intention of heading in that direction.

My first day, I reported for work. My boss gave me a small job to estimate and on his way out said to me, just take messages and I will call you later. He left and a few minutes later the telephone rang; I was frightened to death. I answered the phone and I thought I handled it well, at least I thought so. About ten minutes later the phone rang again. I picked up the phone; the person callings said, "This is the accountant. I will be in your office tomorrow morning at eight o'clock". Subsequently, my boss called in for messages and I told him what the accountant said. This is odd, he said, accountants don't show up at that early in the morning. With great hesitation, I assured him that was what the accountant said.

The next morning, I showed up at my usual time, 9a.m.. There was my boss sitting in his chair waiting for the accountant. At about 9:30, my boss called the accountant who said he never called. I have no idea who it was that called, and still don't. These are the kind of frustrations that a newcomer encounters in a new country. My boss didn't fire me, just the opposite he was rather pleased with my progress. Every once in a while he would bring up his daughter, telling me how great she is, but he finally realized that I wasn't interested. Things were working out well. I became more confident with what I was doing. I could even do my homework in the office at times, and of course, attend school.

Suddenly on June 25, 1950 the Korean War broke out. I registered with the Selective Service, took my physical and was classified 1-A. Needing one more semester to graduate high school, I tried to get a deferment, but I found out, much to my regret, that deferments are granted to college students only.

On February 1, 1951, I was on a bus bound for Fort Devens, Massachusetts, with a bunch of other guys from the New York City area. Sitting next to me was Ted Azrak, a second generation Syrian. He was friendly and we had an interesting conversation on the bus. We arrived at Fort Devens about 11p.m. and were immediately led into barracks. A private first class, acting like a general, showed us how to make a hospital corner on the bunk we were going to sleep in. As he was leaving, he said reveille is at 5:30. I asked Ted what is reveille, he said you will find out at 5:30 in the morning. Perhaps he thought I was kidding.

At 5:30 sharp the lights were turned on, a whistle blasted the silence and the sergeant announced in an unmistakably clear and loud voice, "Fall out". Fall out? "What does fall out mean," I asked Ted. "Get dressed in a hurry and follow the crowd," he said. I saw guys running out of the barracks, half dressed. It was freezing outside at this time of the year. Dawn was barely breaking as I ran out and the sergeant yelled out, 'Fall in". What does fall in mean? I began to get the drift. It was learning things on the job, fast.

We underwent all sorts of tests to get our classification for assignment and were fitted for uniform. At some point the sergeant announced that there would be a GI party on Friday. It sounded good; I didn't know what to expect. The party turned out to be a cleaning detail for the barracks and latrine with a bucket, a mop and detergent.

Within a few days, we shipped out by train to Camp Stewart, Georgia for basic training. The weather was nice and warm during the day but the nights were unmercifully cold. We lived in tents; some of the guys used six blankets to keep warm. Some of the younger guys were very unhappy; they missed their homes, their parents. The cadre didn't help the situation, they were tough. I recall the overnight bivouac, how some of the guys could not handle it. They would complain about their feet being tired; they reported sick just to get out of the trip. Some were just complaining incessantly; some were just crying. Having gone through my experiences in the forest not that long ago at a much younger age, I was taken aback by what I was hearing. Suddenly, I had a flash back when I carried a heavy load of food on my shoulders at night in fear, not knowing when I would be caught, which meant certain death. But here I was in my adopted country, free and proud to be a member equal under the law with every one else. That was a great feeling.

I would often get into discussions with Ted, who was of Syrian decent, who would tell me openly that he hated Jews because they were killing his Syrian brothers. I attempted to present a different point of view, which I thought made more sense. But politics aside, we got along very well.

One day several of the guys from our tent went to church, when they returned, they had some sort of a disagreement about a certain procedure that took place in the church. They came to ask my opinion. I told them that I couldn't help them because I was Jewish. From that point on, some of those guys were still friendly with me, others just wrote me off. They wouldn't talk to me; if I started a conversation, they would simply ignore me, or walk away from me. I had encountered bigots before. I had lived among bigots all my life, whether on a local, community or national level. But this time I felt differently; I was a member of a unit with all rights and privileges under the law. I didn't care if those haters liked me or hated me. I was able to ignore them and not internalize such episodes, as I might have done before.

There were other guys who wanted to be my friend who were helpful in spite of the fact I was foreign born and spoke with an accent. I befriended several guys and we would have a good time together. I recall one guy who was from Texas and spoke with a southern accent. At first I had difficulties understanding him but then I got used to it. His name was Arnold, a real fun guy. I still remember some of his sayings. "Do not count the juvenile of poultry before the proper process of incubation has been fully materialized," which, in simple language, meant "don't count your chickens before they're hatched. Another one: "Not being informed to the highest degree of accuracy I hate to articulate for the fear I might deviate from the truest path of rectitude," which meant, I hate to make a statement about something that I am not too well informed.

As a part of basic training, we would watch battle films, psychological film and other training films. There was one film I'll never forget. It had an enormous impact on me. The film began with a soldier going on furlough and seeing his mother. There came a flashback. When I was about seven, a young guy from the village was called to serve in the Polish army. After basic training he came home on furlough and one day he came to visit us. I was very impressed with the uniform, the bayonet and whatever else he had on as a soldier. I admired him; I clung to him; he let me play with the bayonet. As a young kid I was elated. He talked to my mom and I heard my mom saying to him, "I wish I could live to see my son in uniform like you." I remembered that statement. So, when I was watching that film about the soldier going on furlough and how his mother greeted him, I completely lost my composure. I was crying like a baby, I just couldn't stop. I knew my mother would wasn't waiting to greet me. The guys sitting next to me wanted to know what happened. I later told them my story; some of them understood and were very sympathetic.

After basic training our unit was assigned to a little fort called Fort Banks in Winthrop, Massachusetts, right outside of Boston. I spent the rest of my army career there.

Because of my knowledge of languages, I was tested and passed Polish, Russian, Ukrainian and German and was assigned to intelligence to be dropped behind enemy lines in case of war. I needed a clearance from the FBI because I wasn't a citizen at the time. I qualified, but I couldn't go to OCS (Officer's Candidate School) for the very same reason—not being a citizen. Being in the service didn't qualify me to automatically become a citizen. In the meantime, pending my clearance from the FBI, I was assigned to personnel.

I recall one weekend I came to New York to see my friends and they all asked me whether I was in trouble. FBI men were asking all sorts of questions about me. For a moment I was surprised but then I realized what it was. The clearance finally came through about two months before my discharge in February 1953.

At that point I decided to seek a college education. After my discharge, I had to go back to high school for one more semester to meet the requirements for admission to college. I applied, matriculated and was admitted to New York City College.

With the benefits under the GI Bill of Rights and working part time for Mr. Kirschner who kept the job open, I was able to attend college during the day as well as summer school. This enabled me to graduate City College in three years—Cum Laude—with a degree of Bachelor of Business Administration in 1957 and subsequently became a CPA (Certified Public Accountant).

Right after graduation I got a job as an accountant, but at the same time I also entertained the idea of building my own accounting practice. Soon my dream of having my own practice began to materialize. Tatko, my companion in the forest, now known as A. Liebhart, became my client. He owned a sheet metal shop. Avrum Feiler who owned a butcher store also became my client. Another person who purchased real estate for business became my client. These were relatively small clients, but nevertheless a beginning.

In 1962, instead of going on vacation with friends to the Catskill Mountains as we usually did, I decided to take a trip to Israel to visit my cousins. There I met Ruth, a pretty Sabra. We were married five weeks later and came to the United States. Within two years to the day of our wedding anniversary, September 17, 1964, we had three children, a son named Ron and twin daughters, Leora and Sheira. Being a father to them, bringing them up and watching them grow, I felt blessed far beyond the usual blessing of parenthood. However, as joyous occasions as they were, they were overshadowed by the fact that my parents, especially my mother and sister, weren't there to share the joy with us.

Perhaps they were.

With wonder we saw our children through school, college and beyond. They gave me a world I had never dared hope for. My son has become a computer consultant. My daughters got married and have blessed me with five grandchildren. It never dawned on me in my darkest days in the forest that so many lives would continue through me. Two generations (and hopefully many more) have come into being from what seemed like nothing at all; we are a beautiful family that was almost destroyed to the root by the Nazis.

Unfortunately my marriage to Ruth ended in divorce. It was sad that it had to happen. We just had too many irreconcilable differences.

I had been telling my children about my life experiences. I divided them into short stories, starting when they were very young, about seven or eight, on their level of understanding. As they grew older my stories took on a deeper meaning. At times, they would ask me to tell them more and more. When they grew considerably older I would tell them about our family, especially about my mom; I would get very emotional with tears in my eyes and they would share those moments with me and cry. My son and my daughters are now grown, my daughters have children of their own. They would often bring up the topic; how proud my mother, their grandmother, would be of her grandchildren and her great-grandchildren. We all wind up with tears in our eyes.

My children sometimes suggest that perhaps we should consider going to the place where I spent my childhood and the horrible years during WWII. I had thought about it a number of times, but I don't see much sense in it. Other than seeing the physical location and what it looks like now: the house where we lived, the river where I fished, the places where I picked berries with my sister, the place where we played with other children—none would be the same. Most of the people that I knew or knew me probably have passed on. Those that were still alive would hardly add anything to what I already know. I saw that this kind of visit would only bring about very painful memories of the past.

Eventually I merged my firm with another accounting firm and in 1998 I sold my practice and retired.

What happened to some of the people I spent time with in the forest? (The name in parentheses denotes the name used in the U.S.).

Moyshe (Moses) Hans married Blime shortly after the war ended. They immigrated to the United States and settled in New York. They had three children. Moyshe worked in a luncheonette and subsequently purchased it. Moyshe passed away in the late 80s and Blime passed on a number of years later.

Srul Hans met a woman in the DP camp, married her and immigrated to Argentina. He passed away in the late 60s.

Avrum (Abe) Feiler married Alis after the war. They lived in Brooklyn; had one daughter. Alis died rather young of some sort of a disease. Avrum owned a butcher store and subsequently remarried.

David Berg married Elke shortly after liberation. They settled in New York City. David owned a butcher store. They had four children, a number of grandchildren and great-grandchildren. He retired a few years ago.

Aron Hans married Feige right after the war. They ultimately settled in New York City and had twin daughters. Aron passed away about fifteen years ago. Feige is enjoying her daughters and her grandchildren.

Mordche (Mark) Weicher married Sonia. They finally settled on Long Island. They had one daughter. Unfortunately, he passed away several years ago. Sonia spends time mostly in Florida and enjoys her daughter and her grandchildren.

Isaac (Irving) Weicher married Blossom in the early sixties. They had two children and grandchildren. Unfortunately Blossom passed on. He enjoys his children and grandchildren. He graduated from the City College of New York, spent most of his life in accounting and is semi-retired.

Avrum (Abe) Liebhart (also known as Tatko) married Marcia, a girl from Turka. They had two daughters. Tatko owned a sheet metal business. Unfortunately, he passed away about 15 years ago. Marcia lives in Westchester close to her daughters and grandchildren.

Moynie (Morris) Breitbart married Rose after the war. They had two sons and grandchildren. Moynie spent most of his time in the United States as manager working for Ratner's Restaurant. Unfortunately, Moynie passed away over a year ago.

Mendel Feller, his wife and his two brothers emigrated to Israel right after the war.

Esther wound up on a kibbutz and subsequently, with hard work, earned a Ph.D. Esther married and had three sons. The two sisters Estie and Chavele were left in the orphanage home. Neither Moyshe Hans nor Avrum Feiler nor anybody else followed up on the welfare of the girls. The conclusion was, they remained in Poland and no one knows what became of them.

As for Itzik Operman and Srul Singer and their wives, after we left Turka no one heard from them again.

As of the most recent editing of this book, I was sad to learn that David Berg passed away at the age of 91. He died just after Yom Kippur 2004, 60 years after we were liberated.

FINIS

Tribute

✦

To our father, from your loving children

Sometimes we wonder what the world would've been like today had Hitler and his genocidal army never existed. The dichotomy of emotions is overwhelming – on the one hand knowing that millions of innocent victims, including you and your family, would have been spared the atrocity of the Nazis, yet on the other hand knowing that we would not be here. It's hard to reconcile sometimes.

However, choosing to accept life as it is, we see the good that has come out of all the suffering. First and foremost, your inspirational story of courage which continues to imbue our entire family with faith and purpose. Secondly, your beautiful (if we do say so ourselves), loving and devoted family – a family that is an extension of you; an extension that will continue for generations to come because of your determination to live. And, finally, the message you have sent to the world over and over again – that good will conquer over evil. Every time. You have, through your words, your actions and your wisdom, taught your children tolerance, compassion, honesty, perseverance, joy and presence - - the opposite of what was shown to your family. We live these attributes every day and have made a conscious decision to pass them on to our children, who will live those values and ultimately pass them on to their children and so on and so on. You may not realize the impact that your experience will have on humanity, just as the butterfly doesn't realize how the fluttering of his wings in a certain pattern will cause a tornado on the other side of the hemisphere.

Many children of survivors are often left to wonder what their parent went through because of their inability to talk about the horror. You, however, were not only willing and able to share every detail, but were also able to cry and show us unabashedly how you were affected. We truly cannot convey the impact that you have had and continue to have on our lives but we can thank you from the depths of our souls for all the love, strength and guidance you have given us. And in thanking you we also thank and honor all of those who helped you survive. The Ukranian farmer who hid you in his house only to be hanged a few weeks later in front of his wife and children; the couple who hid with you who were forced to kill their newborn son because his wailing cries would have disclosed your whereabouts; the villagers of Turka who ensured your survival by giving you food and amenities; your co-survivors who provided companionship and encouragement during the scariest time of your life and most importantly…

….your mother, a woman who is the epitome of selflessness, devotion and love. The woman whose maternal instinct would save your life and ultimately give us ours. We thank you most of all, Henya.

We know this book will be an heirloom in our family, increasing in value as it's passed on from generation to generation. Thank you for putting your experience into words and those words onto pages and, in the process, inspiring all of us to believe in miracles, in the power of survival, in the notion that the 'bullets aren't real' and ultimately - - in the power of love.

Daddy, when we were little we thought you were the best, the smartest, the funniest, the most loving father that ever lived.

Now that we're older, we know it.

We love you.
Ron
Leora
Sheira

Maps

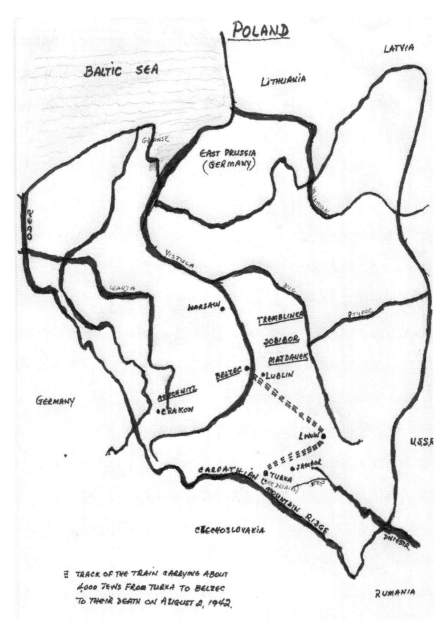

TRACK OF THE TRAIN CARRYING ABOUT
4,000 JEWS FROM TURKA TO BELZEC
TO THEIR DEATH ON AUGUST 2, 1942.

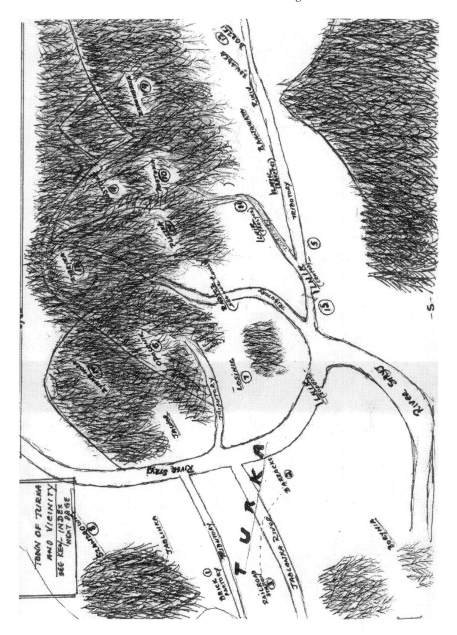

Key Index to Carpathian Mountain Ridge (Turka Area)

1. Approximately 500 Jews were caught in a dog-like fashion by the Gestapo assisted by Ukranian police, taken outside of town and executed.

2. The Germans ordered the Je4ws of Turka and surroundings to report to the barracks for "resettlement" to a labor camp on August 1, 1942.

3. On August 2, 1942, the Jews in the barracks were forced to march to the railroad station, without their belongings, and transported by train to the Belzec death camp and immediately killed.

4. Built the first bunker in the forest for the preparation of hiding. December 1, 1942 was declared to be "Judenfrei" free of Jews.

5. I was caught by the Germans on November 17, 1942.

6. We moved from the bunker to a new location called Opolonik, for fear of being discovered.

7. We killed a farmer who was out to find us or catch us.

8. We killed a farmer, wounded his accomplice and burned down his house. They were out to find us or catch us and collect rewards from the Germans.

9. We moved to a new location, Zadowbana forest, for fear we may have been discovered.

10. The Germans attacked early on March 17, 1944.

11. The Germans killed a farmer in front of his children, accused of helping Jews.

12. We robbed a farmer in fall of 1943.

13. We robbed a farmer in May 1944.

14. Our two groups separated. Some stayed in Plishka, some went to Zymna Hora.

15. On the first day of liberation we stayed at David Berg's house.

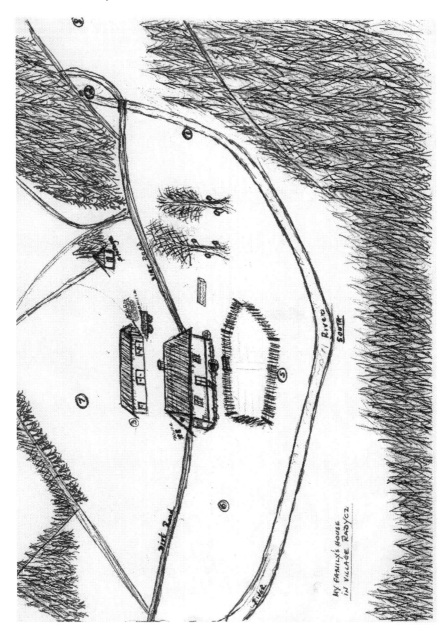

My Family's House in Village Radycz

Key Index to our house (#8) in Radycz

1. I caught my first trout with my bare hands.

2. Cold water spring – extremely cold

3. Barn and stable.

4. The back of the house.

5. My mom's garden, growing strawberries, carrots and a variety of vegetables.

6. Land for growing oats, wheat, etc…

7. Land for growing potatoes.

8. Land for grazing cows, sheep, goats and the horse.

9. The road was a dirt road.

10. The entire village was surrounded by mountains and forests.

11. There were apple trees, cherry trees, pear trees, hazelnut trees, wild strawberries, blueberries and raspberries on our farm.

12.

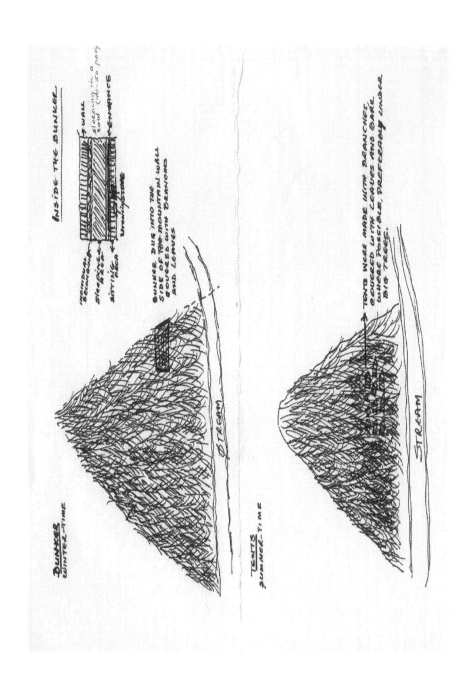

INSIDE THE BUNKER

wall
sleeping in a row (25-30 men)
benches

BUNKER DUG INTO THE SIDE OF THE MOUNTAIN WALL, COVERED WITH BRANCHES AND LEAVES.

STREAM

BUNKER
WINTER-TIME

TENTS WERE MADE WITH BRANCHES, COVERED WITH LEAVES AND BARK WHERE POSSIBLE, PREFERABLY UNDER BIG TREES.

STREAM

TENTS
SUMMER-TIME

152

From Out of the Shadow

The Journey Back To My Childhood Home

✦

August 2, 2009

After my liberation and emigration to the U.S., I vowed never to return to that cursed land, a place where my young life was turned upside down in the blink of an eye. I lost my beautiful family and almost lost my own life.

Many years have past since, and I often think of the pleasant times I had as a youngster. I will always remember and cherish my mother until my dying days. The love and confidence she instilled in me helped me survive the Holocaust, and carried me throughout my life, allowing me to get an education, raise a family and be the man I am today.

I often shared my experiences with my children as they were growing up. Naturally, I kept the details simple in the beginning, but as they grew so did their understanding as I shared more and more of my painful memories. My children learned what my life was like before the war, much of what I went through during the Holocaust, and of course my subsequent years.

I retired in 2001. For years my kids would bring up the idea of visiting my childhood home. Early on, I would avoid discussing the topic, but as time went on I started to change my mind. When Leon Gleicher went to Poland with his children, and then David Berg with his kids, I began to seriously consider this monumental trip. Curiosity started getting the better of me and the truth is I really wanted to be there when my children saw it firsthand.

When I finally made the decision to go, I began to think a lot about my life as a little boy: the house, the stream, the hills, the food bunker across the street (which cooled in the summertime and warmed in the winter), the trees, my mother's garden, the children in the neighborhood, playing with my sister...all my precious childhood memories.

Next thing I knew, I was calling the travel agent David Berg used. I was now committed. When I made the announcement to my children and my fiancé, Mickie, that we were actually going to the Ukraine and Poland, we were all very excited -- and a bit apprehensive.

I started thinking about the languages I once spoke fluently, just like any other Ukrainian or Polish native. I realized I needed to practice the kinds of sentences I would need in order to communicate. I was surprised by how much I forgot and was concerned that I wouldn't be able to express myself. So I bought a Ukrainian/English dictionary. It didn't help. The words didn't make sense to me. They seemed foreign. I guess too many years had gone by.

Our trip began on August 1, 2009. The seven of us (my son, my daughters, their spouses, my fiancé and me) left from from JFK and arrived in Lviv, Ukraine on August 2nd. Unbelievably, and perhaps karmically, August 2nd 1942 was the day I lost my entire family.

Our tour guide, Michael, spoke English very well, which was a big plus. I was continuously befuddled by the fact that I needed help to communicate in my native tongue...to talk with the people in the area in which I grew up.

On August 3rd, sixty seven years later, we were on our way to Radycz, the village of my childhood. Radycz is located next to the village Ilnik and about three miles from a "big" little town called Turka. Once we left the hotel in Lviv, it took over two hours to get even close to Turka. As we approached Ilnik, I looked for houses that I expected to recognize from my childhood. It all seemed strange and unidentifiable. But I sensed that we were getting closer to my village. Some locals told us that we were about half a kilometer from Radycz. I started to get emotional. Nothing seemed familiar. We reached a fork where two small brooks merged. It jogged my memory. We turned right. I knew my house should be on the right. When we drove past the Church (a landmark that I <u>did</u> recognize) I knew we had passed my house without the slightest trace of recognition.

Me speaking with Nikolay Markovicz's son, Vladimir.

We stopped to talk to a farmer. I asked him if he knew someone named Nikolay Markowicz, the man who was the head of the village in 1942. He informed us, to my shock and amazement, that Nikolay was his father. We were speaking to Vladimir Markowicz, who was now 73 years old. I asked if he remembered a Jewish family living in the village and he said, "yes…they had a son called Abrom." He kept repeating that name "Abrom, Abrom". I said, "<u>I</u> am Abrom". Vladimir was somewhat surprised but didn't show much emotion. He brought us to my house that we had passed just moments ago.

No wonder I didn't recognize it at first. The house was abandoned, dilapidated, with no window or doors; the roof was broken and bent in several different directions. My mother's gardens in front and back of the house were overgrown with weeds. And what used to be a barn/ stable that housed our cows, horse, goats, sheep, chickens, turkeys, hay, grain, etc…was now a heap of rotted wood. What served as our refrigerator and storage when I was a little boy was now nothing more than a tiny hill covered with grass. There were houses there that hadn't been there before and they were all on what used to be <u>our</u> land.

Everything had changed so drastically. And it was very disorienting.

I walked around and assessed the property first because I couldn't bring myself to look in the house yet.

After a few nervous minutes I was ready. I walked inside and felt a sadness wash over me. What I was staring at used to be a vibrant, love-filled home. A place where mom and the handmaid would milk the cows, then turn it into cheese and butter. My father, who sold tobacco to local farmers, was also a lumber broker. He would employ laborers to thresh the oats and cut lumber for cooking. But that all died the day they vanished.

Me in front of my childhood home.

What stood before me was nothing like I had remembered. The porch was gone. The once wooden floor was now just dirt. The kitchen where my mom cooked and baked was reduced to rubble. What remained of the living room were four damaged walls. The bedroom where I almost killed my sister with my father's gun (see chapter 2) was in ruins. And the attic, where I spent hours looking through my father's WW1 memorabilia with my sister, was also ravaged with time.

The only thing that remained intact was the spring near the house where my mother used to send me with a bucket to get clean, fresh cold water. The water was still cold and clean.

Everything seemed smaller too. The house, the barn, the stream, even the dirt road appeared narrower. The terrain all around us seemed to have shifted and readjusted in every way.

My house: #8, Village Radycz.

Our barn across the street.

While soaking it all in with disbelief, I ran into an older farmer who was looking for his cow (we're talking very rural village!). I asked him about the neighbors -- I even remembered their names – and he told me they were all dead.

In the midst of this depressing and lifeless vision, a comforting feeling came over me. I felt my mother's presence. I was glad my children were with me because I felt that she sensed them and that she was pleased. I'm sure it was psychological but the feeling of her being there with us was very uplifting and powerful for me.

The kitchen where my mother baked challah for Shabbat.

The one thing I was hoping to recover was our old pictures. My mother, before she left, gave some of our belongings, including the pictures, to our immediate neighbor for safekeeping. The neighbor's house was gone, they were all deceased and they had no children. I lost all hope of ever seeing those pictures again.

I felt like Rip-Van-Winkle waking up sixty-seven years later and seeing how much things had changed -- and not for the better. How did it all go down the drain?

The forest: my home for two years.

My children and Mickie have heard quite a lot about the forests, the bunkers and events associated with it. They wanted to go into the forest and get up-close and experience what it may have felt like. The problem was that the weather was not cooperating and also after all these years, I doubted very much if I could find the exact location of the bunkers. What we did was get very close to the edge of the forest (the Carpathian mountain ridge) and zoom in with our video camera to get a closer look.

My children and me overlooking my house.

I also wanted to leave some time to see the town of Turka. This was the "shtetl" which was part of my life, where I attended public school and, of course, the Jewish school called "cheder". But more importantly, I wanted to show everyone the place where our family (and many others) was tricked into believing that they were being resettled to another place for work. They were told to report to the army barracks (built by the Soviets) in Turka. On August 2nd 1942, the entire town was surrounded by the Gestapo and the Ukrainian police who forced all the Jews to march to the railroad station about two miles away. From there, all of the victims were taken in cattle cars to Belzec Death Camp, where they were immediately murdered.

*The Turka Train Station where my parents and sister were shoved
into cattle cars and taken to Belzec Death Camp.*

As we approached Turka, I saw no trace of the barracks. I couldn't
believe my eyes. We then went to the railroad station and tried to retrace

the road back to the barracks. Turka, like Radycz, had undergone many changes, that didn't allow me to recognize any of the streets. After questioning the police and local residents, we managed to get to the railroad station. It remained intact and in good condition. As I walked the platform I stood there in disbelief, that sixty-seven years ago my family was being loaded onto cattle cars on this very spot. I couldn't wrap my brain around that reality. It was a horrifying, yet somehow sacred moment to be standing there in awe all those years later.

From the railroad station I wanted to go to the barracks, only to find out that they don't exist anymore. Afterwards, I proceeded to find the 'cheder' (children's school) where I was a student. I met two men who lived in the area. One of them told me that his mother had pointed out that this building was once a Jewish school….a long, long time ago.

I must admit that the way Turka looked was very disappointing. What was once a vibrant, clean little town with electric street lights and impressive stores -- mostly owned by Jews -- was now dirty, disheveled, disorganized and dilapidated. It felt like a dead town with living corpses walking around, everyone minding their own business. I didn't see a single smile on any of the faces.

At this point, with it being late afternoon, we decided to return to Lviv because we were visiting Belzec the next day and I knew it was going to be heavy. The following morning we drove to Belzec and met our new Polish tour guide at the entrance to the death camp. Approaching the entrance gates gave me chills. I was trembling as I entered the grounds where sixty-seven years ago, almost to the day, my entire family was wiped out within hours. I was standing on the grounds where my mother, father and sister, whom I loved and adored, met their brutal death.

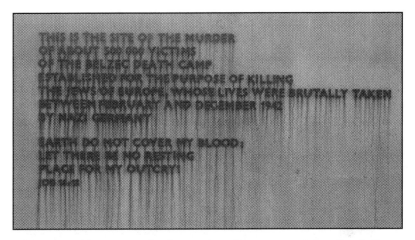

This is the commemoration on the outside wall as you enter Belzec Death Camp.

A guide inside the camp showed us around and gave us a little history of this relatively unknown death camp. The construction started in November 1941 and was completed in February 1942. By March Belzec was ready to receive the first transports. The trains came from different areas in the southern part of Poland. The transport of approximately 4,000 Jews, including my family, was shipped from Turka to the Belzec Death Camp on August 2, 1942.

Since it was one of the first death camps, Belzec was established to carry out experiments to determine the most efficient method of handling the victims from the time of their arrival at the camp until their murder and burial.

The Belzec Death Camp Memorial.

The perimeter of the memorial shows the transport's city of origin.

The month and year is shown as well.

The guide showed us the huge mass grave where there were between five and seven layers of bodies, each covered with dirt. All around this large cemetery were names of towns where the Jews came from. I saw the inscription of Turka with a date August 1942. For years the Polish government would not allow a memorial to this unspeakable tragedy. But today, over half a century later, thanks to a handful of caring Jews, there is a memorial site and museum with a display of pictures as well as books denoting what happened in Belzec. My book "Hiding in Death's Shadow" is now a permanent addition to the Belzec library. One last thing to ponder: the trees all along the perimeter are the only remaining witnesses to one of the greatest crimes committed in the history of humanity.

As we stood at that huge mass grave where 600,000 Jews were slaughtered, my daughters read poems they composed which are incorporated herein. To me, hearing those poems was extremely emotional, especially in this devastating place. There are no words to express what I experienced that day.

We stayed overnight in the town of Lublin, which is not too far from Belzec. The next day we were on our way to Krakow, the city where Auschwitz and Birkenau concentration camps were built.

These infamous extermination camps were a hell that no human should ever witness. Actually seeing it, I could hardly believe what the Nazis were able to perpetrate. Who could have ever imagined that the Germans, at the time considered to be the most educated and sophisticated nation in Europe (if not the world), were capable of transforming themselves into a people of wickedness, evil and horror? One of the most incredulous deeds was to promulgate laws to annihilate a certain group of people. Jews. Standing on the grounds we witnessed the results of that law. It actually made me sick to think that not only were these people murdered, but every part of their bodies was utilized. Their hair was used for mattress stuffing. Their fat was used to make soap. And whatever was left over was cremated and the ashes used as fertilizer. The personal belongings taken from the victims like shoes, clothing, glasses etc. were stored. It was unbearable to see this all with my own eyes.

As difficult as this trip was, revisiting what happened sixty seven years ago was not just emotionally draining, it was also somehow cathartic. I was very pleased that I was able to share this experience with Mickie and my children; it is something I will never forget. Throughout the trip, I felt the presence of my family, as if I were paying them a long overdue visit.

My children and grandchildren.

I have, in essence, two families. My old family of mother, father and sister. And my new family...Mickie, my children, and grandchildren. This visit to the Ukraine and Poland brought my two families together; they are now forever connected in a bond of love, pain, gratitude and forgiveness.

A letter written by Sheira and a poem by Leora were read during the visit. I am concluding this section with these creative pieces that moved me beyond words.

Sheira's Letter:

We are here today to celebrate life
The life that was saved
The lives that were given
The lives that are being lived

Dad, your courage, your bravery, your spirit
Have all led you to this day
They have led you home

We stand here in awe of what this day means
Our history stares us in the face

All the horrors you experienced
May they be forgiven
May a new space open up
A space for tolerance, compassion and love to thrive

Through you, Dad, new life has sprung
And where there is life, there is always hope – hope for a better world
But let us not forget those who are no longer alive
Though they are not on this earth, they are still present
Stop and feel them. They are here.
Let us thank them and remember them with joy.

I hope this experience reminds each of us of the sacredness and fragility of life...
to not take our loved ones for granted and to continue to strive
for peace in our hearts and minds.

Leora's Poem

Sacred is this moment here with you

TO WALK ALONG THE SAME PATH THAT YOU DID

TO SEE THE TREES THAT SAVED YOU AS YOU HID

TO WITNESS WITH MY OWN EYES WHERE YOU GREW

Sacred is this moment here with you

TO SEE THE KITCHEN WHERE YOUR MOTHER COOKED

TO SEE THE TROUT THAT SWAM INSIDE THE BROOK

TO WALK AROUND THE VILLAGE THAT YOU KNEW

Sacred is this moment here with you

WE'RE HERE WITH YOU AND YET YOU WERE THE ONE

WHO WAS THE BROTHER AND THE ONLY SON

WHOSE LIFE WAS CHANGED FOREVER AUGUST 2

Sacred is this moment here with you

YOU HAD A LIFE WITH THEM FOR 14 YEARS

AND SINCE THEY'RE GONE YOU'VE SHED A MILLION TEARS

YOU LOST IT ALL BECAUSE YOU WERE A JEW

Sacred is this moment here with you

I'VE SAID IT BUT I'LL SAY IT ONCE AGAIN

IT'S AN HONOR TO BE YOUR DAUGHTER AND YOUR FRIEND

MAY THIS TRIP BRING YOU HEALING THAT IS NEW

A CONNECTION THAT IS SO LONG OVERDUE

AND KNOW THAT THEY ARE SITTING WITH US TOO

Sacred is this moment here with you